ARIAS FOR
SOPRANO

Volume 2

Compiled and Edited by
Robert L. Larsen

Editorial Advisor: Richard Walters
Assistant Editor: Christopher Ruck

On the cover: "L'opéra de Paris" by Raoul Dufy
Used by permission of The Phillips Collection, Washington D.C.

ISBN 0-634-07868-2

www.schirmer.com
www.halleonard.com

G. SCHIRMER, Inc.

DISTRIBUTED BY

HAL•LEONARD®
CORPORATION
7777 W. BLUEMOUND RD. P.O. BOX 13819 MILWAUKEE, WI 53213

FOREWORD

This is a second compilation of arias for lyric soprano, completed well over a decade after the publication of the first soprano volume in the *G. Schirmer Opera Anthology*. Many of the selections fall within the compass of a gifted student, but all of them are worthy of the greatest artists of any age. Again, the plan has been to avoid the heavier dramatic literature of Verdi, Wagner, Puccini and others of the veristic composers.

This volume clearly points up the fact that there are many kinds of soprano voices that are basically lyric in nature. Probably the voice that sings the definitive "Je suis encor" is not the one to be at home in "Ebben?... Ne andrò lontana," but then I've known a very few who could do it all.

I listen to literally hundreds of soprano arias in auditions for the Des Moines Metro Opera every year, so I hear many of these arias often. Some arias which are very valuable as learning tools, or as musical and stylistic challenges for recital, are not necessarily the best vehicles with which to showcase a talent in an opera audition. My soundest advice for audition purposes is to discover those pieces which show you and your voice to the very best advantage... and shorter is always better than longer.

Bringing these disparate pieces together under one cover has brought the personal satisfaction that as a coach I will not have to hunt frantically for the copy of "Chi il bel sogno di Doretta" or "Marietta's Lied" that seems to have disappeared from the studio again. The rich variety of this literature discovers almost all of the greatest opera composers in some of their most inspired moments.

Enjoy!

Robert L. Larsen
May, 2004

CONTENTS

NOTES and TRANSLATIONS

The arias are presented chronologically by year of first performance.

GIULIO CESARE
(Julius Caesar)
1724
music by George Frideric Handel
libretto by Nicola Francesco Haym (after history and legend)

Non disperar

from Act I, scene 5
setting: Egypt, 48 BCE; Cleopatra's palace
character: Cleopatra

The action of this opera is based on Julius Caesar's visit to Egypt in 48-47 B.C. where he met Cleopatra. He was 54 at the time but this opera seems to portray him much younger.

The Egyptian army has been defeated by Julius Caesar. Cleopatra has just discovered that her brother, with whom she loathes to share the throne of Egypt, has just sent Caesar the head of his rival Pompey in a basket. Cleopatra is horrified and tells Ptolemy to concentrate on his harem of "pretty ones." He will have far more luck in love than in negotiating with Caesar.

Anzi tu pur, effeminato amante,	*On the contrary, it is you, effeminate lover,*
va dell' età sui primi nati albori,	*You, still in the dawn of your life,*
di regno invece a coltivar gli amori!	*Forsaking your kingdom to pursue your loves!*
Non disperar, chi sa?	*Do not despair, who knows?*
se al regno non l'avrai,	*You might achieve the success in reigning,*
avrai sorte in amor.	*that you achieved in love.*
Mirando una beltà	*Looking at your beauty*
in essa troverai	*you discover in it*
a consolar un cor.	*how to calm a heart.*

Piangerò la sorte mia

from Act III, scene 3
setting: Egypt, 48 BCE; Cleopatra's palace
character: Cleopatra

Ptolemy's forces have defeated those of Cleopatra, and she has been taken prisoner. Certain of her death, she bids farewell to her hand-maidens in this moving aria.

E pur così in un giorno	*Therefore in one day*
perdo fasti e grandezze? Ahi, fato rio!	*I lose fame and greatness? Oh, treacherous fate!*
Cesare, il mio bel nume, è forse estinto;	*Caesar, my protector, is perhaps no more;*
Cornelia e Sesto inermi son, nè sanno	*Cornelia and Sesto are powerless,*
darmi soccorso. Oh Dio!	*they cannot assist me. O God!*
Non resta alcuna speme al viver mio.	*No hope remains in my life.*
Piangerò la sorte mia,	*I will lament my destiny,*
sì crudele e tanto ria,	*so cruel and merciless,*
finché vita in petto avrò.	*as long as there is life in my body.*
Ma poi morta d'ogn'intorno	*But once dead, everywhere,*
il tiranno e notte e giorno	*the tyrant, night and day,*
fatta spettro agiterò.	*my spirit will torment.*

LA SERVA PADRONA
(The Maid Turned Mistress)
1733
music by Giovanni Battista Pergolesi
libretto by Gennaro Antonio Federico

Stizzoso, mio stizzoso

from Intermezzo I
setting: Naples, the 18th century; Uberto's house
character: Serpina

La Serva Padrona, an "intermezzo," was first played between the acts of Pergolesi's opera seria *Il prigioniero superbo* and subsequently was performed all over Europe, becoming the subject of great controversy in the "Querelle des Bouffons," ("Quarrel of the comedians") in Paris.

Serpina is the servant of Liberto and also his ward. She has become hard to handle for the old fellow. He thinks that having a wife might improve the situation and orders his servant Vespone to find him one. Serpina becomes irate and insists that he marry her.

Stizzoso, mio stizzoso,	*Cross one, my cross one,*
voi fate il borioso,	*you act haughtily,*
ma non vi può giovare!	*but that will do you no good!*
Bisogna al mio divieto	*You must accept my demand*
star cheto, e non parlare!	*without reply, and remain silent!*
Zit! Serpina vuol così.	*Silence! Serpina commands it.*
Cred'io che m'intendete,	*I think you understand me,*
dacché mi conoscete,	*since you have known me*
son molti e molti dì!	*a very long time!*

ORFEO ED EURIDICE
(Orpheus and Euridice)
1762
music by Christoph Willibald von Gluck
libretto by Raniero de Calzabigi (after Greek myth)

Qual vita è questa mai... Che fiero momento

from Act III, scene 1
setting: mythological Greece; a somber vault in the underworld
character: Euridice

The Shades have delivered Euridice to her beloved husband, Orpheus, permitting him to lead her out of Hades on the condition that he does not look at her on the journey. Euridice is confused and dismayed by his aloofness and refuses to go further if only unrequited love lies before her.

Qual vita è questa mai, che a viver incomincio!	*What sort of life is this, which I am beginning to live!*
E qual arcan m'asconde Orfeo?	*And what secret does Orpheus conceal from me?*
Tratto m'avria dal recesso feral	*Did he draw me out of the funereal place*
per farsi reo del perfido abbandono?	*in order to make himself guilty of the treacherous abandonment?*
Si smentisce la luce, o ciel, agli occhi miei.	*The light is fading, oh heaven, before my eyes.*
Oppresso in seno mi diventa affannoso il respirar.	*Heavy in my breast, my breathing is becoming difficult.*
Tremo... vacillo... e sento fra l'angoscia e il terrore,	*I tremble... I waver... and I feel, among anxiety and terror –*
quando all'ebbrezza, rediviva, aspiro,	*as I long for elation, returned to life –*
da un palpito crudel sento, ahimè! vibrarmi il cor.	*I feel my heart vibrating, alas, from a painful throbbing.*
Che fiero momento!	*What a brutal moment!*
Che barbara sorte!	*What a cruel fate,*
Passar dalla morte a tanto dolor!	*to pass from death to such sorrow.*

Translation by Martha Gerhart

PARIDE ED ELENA

(Paris and Helen)
1770
music by Christoph Willibald von Gluck
libretto by Raniero de Calzabigi

Lo temei... Lo potrò! Ma frattanto, oh infelice

from Act IV
setting: A room in the royal palace of Sparta
character: Elena

Zeus chose the Trojan Paris to judge who was the most beautiful—Juno, Minerva, or Venus, but Paris heard there was yet a more beautiful woman in Sparta. He goes there and discovers Helen. Paris tells her that the gods have promised her to him, but she replies that he has abused laws and customs because she is betrothed to another. In this aria she wavers between the love she feels for the handsome Paris and her duty to Minelaus.

Lo temei: non mi sento in faccia a lui valor che basti.	*I feared it: at the sight of him I do not feel courage enough.*
Appena frenarmi seppi.	*I barely knew how to restrain myself.*
Ero ridotta al punto d'aprirgli,	*I was reduced to the point of opening up to him,*
di svelargli tutta l'anima mia.	*of revealing to him my whole heart.*
Ah, la possiede, vi regna, n'è tiranno;	*Ah, he dominates it, he reigns there, and he is its tyrant;*
e lo conobbe il barbaro e n'abusa.	*and the barbarian recognized that and takes advantage of it.*
Ove m'inoltro! In qual pensier vaneggio,	*Where am I going! With what thoughts am I raving,*
in qual misero error!	*in what miserable deception!*
Si lasci omai alla sola ragion tutto l'impero	*Now let reason alone rule my heart*
che seco ha nel mio core Amor diviso.	*which Cupid has divided.*
Lo potrò! Così voglio! Ho già deciso!	*I shall be able to do it! Thus do I wish! I have now decided!*
Lo potrò! Ma frattanto, oh infelice,	*I shall be able to do it! But meanwhile – oh unhappy me –*
odio ed amo, risolvo e mi pento;	*I hate and I love, I resolve and I repent;*
pietà, sdegno, timore, contento	*pity, disdain, fear, and contentment*
a vicenda mi fanno penar.	*in turn are making me suffer.*
Così voglio! Sì, mentre è lontano,	*Thus do I wish – yes, while he is far away,*
il tiranno che i ceppi me diede;	*the tyrannical one who imposed fetters on me;*
ma se prega, se piange al mio piede,	*yet if he begs, if he weeps at my feet,*
non so più che tacere e tremar!	*I will know only how to be silent and to tremble!*
Lo potrò! Così voglio! Ho deciso!	*I shall be able to do it! Thus do I wish! I have decided!*
Ah, così mi consolo e lusingo;	*Ah, thus do I console and delude myself,*
ma il mio core agitato e diviso,	*but my agitated and divided heart –*
quel che penso, che sogno, che fingo	*what I am thinking, dreaming, and imagining –*
co' suoi moti mi viene a turbar!	*disturbs me with its emotions!*
Oh infelice, odio ed amo, risolvo e mi pento;	*Oh unhappy me – I hate and I love, I resolve and I repent;*
ma il mio core agitato e diviso,	*but my agitated and divided heart –*
quel che penso, che sogno, che fingo	*what I am thinking, dreaming, and imagining –*
co' suoi moti mi viene a turbar!	*disturbs me with its emotions!*

Translation by Martha Gerhart

IDOMENEO

1781
music by Wolfgang Amadeus Mozart
libretto by Abbè Gianbattista Varesco (after ancient legend, and Antoine Danchet's libretto for *Idomenée*, an opera by Antoine Campra)

Zeffiretti lusinghieri

from Act III
setting: Sidon, a port on Crete, *c*1200 BCE, about the end of the Trojan War
character: Ilia

The Trojan wars have ended. Ilia, the daughter of Troy's king Priam, is a captive of the Greek warrior King Idomeneo of Crete. Sent ahead of the king to the island, she falls in love with the king's son, Idamante, and he with her. In this aria she bids the breeze to carry her affection to her beloved.

Solitudini amiche, aure amorose,	*Friendly isolated places, fair winds,*
piante fiorite, e fiori vaghi, udite	*fledgling plants and cherished flowers, listen*
d'una infelice amante	*to a miserable lover's*
i lamenti, che a voi lassa confido.	*laments, to one who, wearied, trusts in you.*
Quanto il tacer presso al mio vincitore,	*How much my silence toward my victor,*
quanto il finger ti costa afflitto core!	*how much the concealment pains you, my grieving heart!*
Zeffiretti lusinghieri,	*Charming breezes,*
deh volate al mio tesoro:	*pray, fly to my dear one,*
e gli dite, ch'io l'adoro,	*and tell him I adore him;*
che mi serbi il cor fedel.	*may he preserve his faithful heart for me.*
E voi piante, e fior sinceri,	*And you, plants and truthful flowers,*
che ora innaffia il pianto amaro,	*which my bitter tears now moisten,*
dite a lui, che amor più raro	*tell him that love more rare*
mai vedeste sotto al ciel.	*you have never seen beneath heaven.*

DIE ENTFÜHRUNG AUS DEM SERAIL

(The Abduction from the Seraglio)
1782
music by Wolfgang Amadeus Mozart
libretto by Gottlieb Stephanie the younger (after a libretto by Christoph Friedrich Bretzner)

Ach, ich liebte, war so glücklich

from Act I
setting: Turkey, the 16th century; the palace of Pasha Selim
character: Konstanze

Konstanze is a Spanish lady who is a captive in the court of Pasha Selim. The Pasha, understandably fascinated by her, has remained respectful and asks why she is so sad and seemingly inconsolable. In this aria she recalls her lost love, and her lament turns into an intense protest against her confinement.

Ach, ich liebte, war so glücklich,	*Ah, I loved, was so lucky,*
kannte nicht der Liebe Schmerz;	*knew not the misery of love;*
schwur ihm Treue, dem Geliebten,	*I swore loyalty to him, my beloved,*
gab dahin mein ganzes Herz.	*giving my entire heart.*
Doch wie schnell schwand meine Freude!	*But how quickly my joy disappeared!*
Trennung war mein banges Los,	*Parting was my cruel destiny,*
und nun schwimmt mein Aug' in Tränen;	*and now my eyes swim in tears;*
Kummer ruht in meinem Schoss.	*Grief rests in my lap.*

COSÌ FAN TUTTE

(Women Are Like That)
1790
music by Wolfgang Amadeus Mozart
libretto by Lorenzo da Ponte

In uomini, in soldati

from Act I

setting: Naples, the 18th century; the house shared by the sisters Fiordiligi and Dorabella
character: Despina

Despina is a chamber maid to two sisters, Fiordiligi and Dorabella, whose soldier lovers have been called away to war, or at least the ladies believe this falsehood of trickery. The ladies are consumed with grief. Despina encourages them to cheer up; after all, even if the lads are killed in battle, there are plenty more men out there from which to choose.

In uomini, in soldati sperare fedeltà?	*In men, in soldiers, to hope for fidelity?*
Non vi fate sentir, per carità!	*Don't let anybody hear you, for pity's sake!*
Di pasta simile son tutti quanti,	*All of them are made of the same paste;*
le fronde mobili l'aure incostanti	*the rustling leaves and inconstant breezes*
han più degli uomini stabilità.	*have more stability than men.*
Mentite lagrime, fallàci sguardi, voci ingannevoli,	*Lying tears, false glances, deceitful voices,*
vezzi bugiardi son le primarie lor qualità.	*charms are their primary qualities.*
In noi non amano che il lor diletto;	*They love us only for their own delight;*
poi ci dispregiano, neganci affetto,	*afterwards they despise us, deny us love;*
nè val da' barbari chieder pietà.	*there is no use asking a barbarian for mercy.*
Paghiam, o femmine, d'ugual moneta	*Let us repay, o women, with the same money*
questa malefica razza indiscreta;	*this evil kind of indiscreet men;*
amiam per comodo, per vanità.	*let us love at our leisure, for our vanity.*

Una donna a quindici anni

from Act II

setting: Naples, the 18th century; the house shared by the sisters Fiordiligi and Dorabella
character: Despina

Fiordiligi and Dorabella are being pursued by Albanians, who are actually their old lovers in disguise. They have thus far rebuffed their dramatic advances, but Dorabella, the younger sister, begins to show some curiosity. Despina offers her own philosophy of love-making and of handling men, and assures them that she can offer more detailed advice if required.

Una donna a quindici anni	*A girl at age fifteen*
dee saper ogni gran moda,	*ought to know all worldly ways:*
dove il diavolo ha la coda,	*all sorts of deceptions,**
cosa è bene, e mal cos'è;	*what is good, and what is bad;*
dee saper le maliziette,	*she ought to know the little tricks*
che innamorano gli amanti,	*that charm lovers:*
finger riso, finger pianti,	*to feign laughter, to feign tears,*
inventar i bei perchè.	*to invent good excuses.*
Dee in un momento dar retta a cento,	*She must pay attention to a hundred men at once,*
colle pupille parlar con mille,	*talk to a thousand with her eyes,*
dar speme a tutti, sien belli o brutti,	*give hope to all, be they handsome or ugly,*
saper nascondersi senza confondersi,	*know how to be secretive without getting flustered,*
senza arrossire saper mentire,	*without blushing, know how to lie,*
e qual regina dall'alto soglio	*and, like a queen from her lofty throne,*
col "posso e voglio" farsi ubbidir.	*with "I can" and "I want," be obeyed.*
Par ch'abbian gusto	*It seems that they're taking a liking*
di tal dottrina;	*to such a doctrine;*
viva Despina,	*long live Despina,*
che sa servir.	*who knows how to be of service!*

*An idiomatic expression; literal translation of the words is "where the devil has his tail."

Translation by Martha Gerhart

LA CLEMENZA DI TITO

(The Clemency of Titus)
1791
music by Wolfgang Amadeus Mozart
libretto by Caterino Mazzolà, adapted from a libretto by Pietro Metastasio

S'altro che lacrime

from Act II
setting: Rome, c. 80 AD
character: Servilia

The Emperor Titus has miraculously escaped a plot on his life initiated by his friend Sextus, but instigated by Vitellia, adored by Sextus but at this moment the Empress-designate. Sextus' sister, Servilia, tells Vitellia in this gentle minuet that weeping alone won't save Sextus' life. She must speak. [Note: The title of this aria is also sometimes "S'altro che lagrime." "Lacrime" and "lagrime" are simply different spellings of the same word, and either is acceptable.]

<table>
<tr>
<td>
S'altro che lacrime per lui non tenti,
tutto il tuo piangere non gioverà.
A questa inutile pietà che senti,
oh quanto è simile la crudeltà.
</td>
<td>
If you don't attempt something other than tears for him,
all your weeping will be in vain.
To this useless pity which you feel,
oh, how similar is cruelty.
</td>
</tr>
</table>

Translation by Martha Gerhart

DER FREISCHÜTZ

(The Free-shooter)
1821
music by Carl Maria von Weber
libretto by Johann Friedrich Kind (after a story by Johann August Apel and Freidrich Laun, and Gothic legend)

Einst träumte meiner sel'gen Base... Trübe Augen

from Act III
setting: Mythical, ancient Germany; Agathe's chamber
character: Ännchen

Ännchen is the charming cousin of Agathe, who is the daughter of the master of the hunt. Agathe hopes that this will be the day she is united in marriage to her beloved Max, but he must first win the shooting competition. Agathe has been haunted by nightmares about being a white dove shot by Max and turned into a bird of prey lying dead in its own blood. Ännchen dismisses it all as inspired by thoughts of her white wedding dress and a feather she saw in Max's hat. Ännchen then tries to cheer her companion up by relating a dream that her cousin once had.

<table>
<tr>
<td>
Einst träumte meiner sel'gen Base,
die Kammerthür eröffne sich,
und kreideweiß ward ihre Nase,
denn näher, furchtbar näher,
schlich ein Ungeheuer, mit Augen wie Feuer,
mit klirrender Kette.
Es nahte dem Bette, in welchem sie schlief –
ich meine die Base mit kreidger Nase –
und stöhnte, ach! so hohl,
und ächzte, ach! so tief!
Sie kreuzte sich, rief,
nach manchem Angst- und Stoßgebet:
Susanne! Margareth'!
Und sie kamen mit Licht, und –
denke nur – und (erschrick mir nur nicht!),
und (graust mir doch!) – und der Geist war:
Nero, der Kettenhund!
</td>
<td>
Once upon a time my late cousin dreamt that
her bedroom door opened,
and her nose turned chalk-white
because closer, ever frighteningly closer,
crept a monster with eyes like fire,
with clanking chains.
It approached the bed in which she was sleeping –
that is, the cousin with chalk-white nose –
and it moaned, ah, so hollowly,
and it groaned, ah, so deeply!
She crossed herself and cried out,
after many an anxious and fervent prayer:
Susan! Margaret!
And they came with lights, and –
just think – and (don't be alarmed!)...
and (though I shudder!) – and the ghost was
Nero, the watch-dog!
</td>
</tr>
<tr>
<td>
Du zürnest mir?
Doch kannst du wähnen, ich fühle nicht mit dir?
Nur zieman einer Braut nicht Thränen.
</td>
<td>
Are you angry with me?
You can't really imagine that I don't feel for you?
But tears are not becoming to a bride.
</td>
</tr>
</table>

Trübe Augen, Liebchen,
taugen einem holden Bräutchen nicht.
Daß durch Blicke sie erquicke und beglücke,
und bestricke, alles um sich her entzücke;
das ist ihre schönste Pflicht.
Lass in öden Mauern Büßerinnen trauern;
dir winkt ros'ger Hoffnung Licht!
Schon entzündet sind die Kerzen
zum Verein getreuer Herzen;
dir winkt ros'ger Hoffnung Licht.
Holde Freundin, zage nicht!

Sad eyes, darling,
are not good for a lovely young bride.
With her glances she should enliven and delight
and charm, enchant everyone around her;
that is her finest duty.
Let penitents mourn within bleak walls;
to you beckons the light of rosy hope!
Already lit are the candles
for the union of true hearts;
to you beckons the light of rosy hope!
Lovely friend, do not be faint-hearted!

Translation by Martha Gerhart

I CAPULETI E I MONTECCHI
(The Capulets and the Montagues)
1830
music by Vincenzo Bellini
libretto by Felice Romani (based on his libretto *Giulietta e Romeo*, an opera by Nicola Vaccai; also based on a tragedy by Luigi Scevola, and Shakespeare's *Romeo and Juliet*)

Oh! quante volte

from Act I

setting: Verona, the 13th century
character: Giulietta

This difficult romanza is one of Bellini's most famous arias. It was adapted from an earlier Bellini opera, *Adelson e Salvini* (a common practice in those days). Romeo's proposed marriage to Giulietta, which would unite their rival houses, has been rejected, and Giulietta is betrothed to Tybalt. Giulietta is tortured by her love for Romeo and the certainty that responding to his advances will cause her and her family pain and tragedy.

Eccomi in lieta vesta... Eccomi adorna...
come vittima all'ara. Oh! almen potessi
qual vittima cader dell'ara al piede!
O nuzïali tede,
abborrite così, così fatali,
siate, ah! siate per me faci ferali.
Ardo... una vampa, un foco
tutta mi strugge. Un refrigerio ai venti
io chiedo invano! Ove sei tu, Romeo?
In qual terra t'aggiri?
Dove, dove inviarti, dove i miei sospiri?

Here I am, dressed brilliantly... Here I am, adorned...
like a victim at the altar. Oh! if only I could
fall like a sacrifice at the base of the altar!
O nuptial flames,
so horrid to me, so fateful,
may you ah! may you be my funeral torches.
I burn... a blaze, a furnace
completely engulfs me. A cooling breeze
I seek vainly! Where are you, Romeo?
To what land have you gone?
Where, where shall I send you my yearning cries?

Oh! quante volte, oh! quante
ti chiedo al ciel piangendo!
Con quale ardor t'attendo,
e inganno il mio desir!
Raggio del tuo sembiante,
ah! parmi il brillar del giorno:
ah! l'aura che spira intorno
mi sembra un tuo sospir.

Oh! how often, oh! very often
I call for you, crying to heaven!
With what ardor I look for you,
and mislead my desire!
A vision of your face,
ah! the sunlight seems to me:
ah! the winds that drift round me
seem to me to be your breath.

LA TRAVIATA
(The Fallen Woman)
1853
music by Giuseppe Verdi
libretto by Francesco Maria Piave (after the play *La Dame aux Camélias* by Alexandre Dumas Fils)

Ah! forse è lui... Sempre libera

from Act I
setting: Paris, 1850; the house where Violetta is living
character: Violetta Valery

The guests have just left the late-night festivities in Violetta Valery's lavish Paris residence. A young and handsome stranger, Alfredo Germont, has appeared at the party and promised to take her away from her frenzied existence and give her real love. She is overwhelmed by this unprecedented dilemma, complicated by her strangely sincere feelings for him. But then her mood changes. She is sure that she is not destined to know that kind of love and that she must live only for the pleasure of the moment. Even Alfredo's passionate serenade from below her window cannot deter her for the moment from her resolve.

È strano!... è strano!... in core	*How odd!... how odd!... on my heart*
scolpiti ho quegli accenti!...	*those words are carved!...*
Sarìa per me sventura un serio amore?	*Would it be so bad if I really fell in love?*
Che risolvi, o turbata anima mia?	*What have you resolved, o tormented soul of mine?*
Null'uomo ancora t'accendeva... o gioia	*No man has yet ignited your passion... o joy*
ch'io non conobbi, esser amata amando!	*I have not known, to love and to be loved!*
E sdegnarla poss'io	*And shall I deny it*
per l'aride follie del viver mio?	*for the barren senselessness of how I now live?*
Ah! forse è lui che l'anima	*Ah! perhaps it could be he whom my soul,*
solinga ne' tumulti,	*alone in the tumult,*
godea sovente pingere	*frequently delighted in depicting*
de' suoi colori occulti!	*in mysterious hues?*
Lui che modesto e vigile	*He, modest and watchful,*
all'egre soglie ascese,	*visited me when I was ill,*
e nuova febbre accese	*and ignited a new fever*
destandomi all'amor.	*by awakening my love.*
A quell'amor che è palpito	*To that love which is the pulse*
dell'universo intero,	*of the whole universe,*
misterioso, altero,	*mysterious, proud,*
croce e delizia al cor!	*pain and delight of the heart!*
Follie! follie! Delirio vano è questo!...	*Madness! madness! This is vain delirium!...*
Povera donna! sola!	*Poor woman! alone!*
abbandonata in questo	*abandoned in this*
popoloso deserto	*crowded wilderness*
che appellano Parigi,	*they call Paris,*
che spero or più? che far degg'io? gioire,	*what more can I hope for? what should I do? I must rejoice,*
di voluttà nei vortici perire!	*must die in a whirlwind of delight!*
Sempre libera degg'io	*Always free must I*
folleggiare di gioia in gioia,	*flit from joy to joy,*
vo' che scorra il viver mio	*I want my life to race*
pei sentieri del piacer.	*along the paths of joy.*
Nasca il giorno o il giorno muoia,	*From dawn to dusk,*
sempre lieta ne ritrovi,	*always merry I will be,*
a diletti sempre nuovi	*toward ever new delights*
dee volare il mio pensier.	*must my thoughts fly.*

LES PÊCHEURS DE PERLES

(The Pearl Fishers)
1863
music by Georges Bizet
libretto by Michel Carré and "Eugène Cormon" (Pierre-Étienne Piestre)

Me voilà seule... Comme autrefois

from Act II
setting: Ceylon, tribal era; the ruins of an Indian Hindu temple
character: Léïla

Léïla is a Brahman priestess who has taken a vow of chastity. Nadir has long loved her but only from a distance and in occasional, longing glances. Still, they both feel drawn to each other. As she spends her first moonlit night alone in the temple, she feels very near to Nadir and knows that this man she adores is watching over her.

Me voilà seule dans la nuit,	*Here I am alone in the night,*
seule en ce lieu désert où règne le silence.	*alone in this deserted place where silence reigns.*
Je frissonne, j'ai peur, et le sommeil me fuit.	*I tremble, I am afraid, and sleep eludes me.*
Mais il est là; mon cœur devine sa présence.	*But he is there; my heart feels his presence.*
Comme autrefois dans la nuit sombre,	*As before, in the somber night,*
caché sous le feuillage épais,	*concealed beneath the dense foliage,*
il veille près de moi dans l'ombre.	*he keeps watch, near me, in the darkness.*
Je puis dormir, rêver en paix.	*I am able to sleep, to dream in peace.*
Il veille près de moi comme autrefois.	*He keeps watch, near me, as before.*
C'est lui! mes yeux l'ont reconnu!	*It's he! My eyes have recognized him!*
C'est lui! mon âme est rassurée!	*It's he! My soul is reassured!*
O bonheur! joie inespérée!	*Oh happiness! Unexpected joy!*
Pour me revoir il est venu.	*To see me again he has come.*
O bonheur! Il est venu.	*Oh happiness! He has come.*
Il est là près de moi, ah!	*He is there, near me, ah!*
Comme autrefois dans la nuit sombre,	*As before, in the somber night,*
caché sous le feuillage épais,	*concealed beneath the dense foliage,*
il veille près de moi dans l'ombre.	*he keeps watch, near me, in the darkness.*
Je puis dormir, rêver en paix.	*I am able to sleep, to dream in peace.*
Il veille près de moi comme autrefois.	*He keeps watch, near me, as before.*
Oui, comme autrefois, je puis rêver, ah! en paix.	*Yes, as before, I am able to dream – ah! – in peace.*

Translation by Martha Gerhart

PRODANÁ NEVÉSTA

(The Bartered Bride)
1866
music by Bedřich Smetana
libretto by Karel Sabina

Och, jaký žal!... Ten lásky sen
(Mařenka's Aria)

from Act III
setting: The village green; near the tavern
character: Mařenka

Mařenka thinks that she has been deserted by Jeník, the man she loves, who seems to have renounced her for a significant sum of money. When Vašek, a simple young man of the village, appears to be the next in line for her hand, she asks to be alone for a few minutes. Her parents argue and urge her to think things over.

Och, jaký žal! jaký to žal,	*Oh, what sorrow! what sorrow!*
když srdce oklamáno!	*when a heart is betrayed!*
Však přece ještě nevěřím,	*But, I still don't accept it,*
ač stojí tam napsáno.	*though it exists there in writing.*
Nevěřím, až s ním promluvím.	*I won't accept it until I talk with him.*
Snad ani o tom neví!	*Perhaps he doesn't even know of it!*
ó, kýž se mi v nesnázi té skutečná,	*Oh, in my shame let the irrefutable,*
skutečná pravda zjeví!	*the irrefutable truth be shown to me!*
Ten lásky sen, jak krásný byl, ten lásky sen,	*This vision of love, how wonderful it was, this vision of love,*
jak krásný byl, jak nadějné rozkvítal!	*how wonderful it was, how faithfully it bloomed!*
A nad ubohým srdcem mým co tichá hvězda svítal,	*And over my distraught heart it was beaming like a silent star,*
Jak blahý život s milencem	*How in this vision an ecstatic life*
v snu tomto jsem si přadla!	*with my love I saw!*
Tu osud přivál vichřici a růže lásky svadla.	*Now destiny rushed in a storm, and love's rose has perished.*
Ne, není možný taký klam, ne, není,	*No, such betrayal is not possible, no, it's not,*
není možný taký klam!	*such betrayal is impossible!*
Tent' smutnou by byl ranou,	*It would be a bitter pain,*
a rozplakala by se zem nad láskou pochovanou,	*and the earth would erupt in tears over the entombed love,*
nad láskou, láskou pochovanou!	*over the entombed love, love!*

DIE FLEDERMAUS

(The Bat)

1870

music by Johann Strauss

libretto by Carl Haffner and Richard Genée (after a French vaudeville, *Le Réveillon*, by Meilhac and Halévy)

Klänge der Heimat

(Csárdás)

from Act II

setting: Vienna, the second half of the 19th century; a ballroom; a lavish party hosted by the Russian Prince Orlofsky

character: Rosalinde

Rosalinde arrives at Orlofsky's ball disguised as a Hungarian countess and announces herself in this grand aria, which follows the Hungarian dance forms of lassu and friska. She knows her husband, who is supposed to be in jail, is at the party. In her mask and elaborate disguise, she fully intends to seduce him and reveal his philandering tendancies.

Klänge der Heimat, ihr weckt mir das Sehnen,	*Sounds of my homeland, you kindle my yearning,*
rufet die Tränen ins Auge mir!	*bringing tears to my eyes!*
Wenn ich euch höre, ihr heimischen Lieder,	*When I hear you, native songs,*
zieht michs wieder, mein Ungarland, zu dir!	*you lure me back, my Hungary, to you!*
O Heimat so wunderbar,	*Oh homeland, so wonderful,*
wie strahlt dort die Sonne so klar!	*how bright is the sunlight there!*
Wie grün deine Wälder, wie lachend die Felder,	*How green are your forests, how joyful are the fields,*
o land, wo so glücklich ich war!	*oh land, I was so happy there!*
Ja, dein geliebtes Bild meine Seele so ganz erfüllt,	*Yes, your beloved vision completely fills my heart,*
dein geliebtes Bild!	*your beloved vision!*
Und bin ich auch von dir weit, ach weit,	*And though I am distant from you, ah so far away,*
dir bleibt in Ewigkeit	*to you I give for all eternity*
doch mein Sinn immer dar, ganz allein geweiht!	*my heart, always there, devoted only to you!*

Feuer, Lebenslust, schwellt echte Ungarbrust,	*Fire, zest for living, swell the real Hungarian chest,*
Heil! Zum Tanze schnell, Csárdás tönt so hell!	*Hurrah! Quickly to the dance, the Csárdás sounds so clearly!*
Braunes Mägdelein musst meine Tänz'rin sein;	*Brown-skinned girl, you must dance with me;*
Reich den Arm geschwind, dunkeläugig Kind!	*Give your arm to me quickly, dark-eyed child!*
Zum Fiedelklingen, ho, ha, tönt jauchzend Singen:	*To the tunes of the fiddle, ho, ha, sounds jubilant singing:*
Mit dem Sporn geklirrt, wenn dann die Maid verwirrt	*With the spurs clanging, and the girl twirling*
senkt zur Erd' den Blick, das verkündet Glück!	*sink to the ground, see the promised good fortune!*
Durst'ge Zecher, greift zum Becher,	*Thirsty drinkers, seize the glass,*
lasst ihn kreisen schnell von Hand zu Hand!	*pass it round quickly from hand to hand!*
Schlürft das Feuer im Tokayer,	*Swig the fire in the Tokay*,*
bringt ein Hoch aus dem Vaterland! Ha!	*raise a toast from the fatherland! Ha!*
Feuer, Lebenslust, schwellt echte Ungarbrust,	*Fire, zest for life, swell the real Hungarian chest,*
Heil! Zum Tanze schnell! Csárdás tönt so hell!	*Hurrah! Quickly to the dance! The Csárdás sounds so clearly!*
La, la, la, la, la!	*La, la, la, la, la!*

*A strong Hungarian wine made from Tokay grapes.

HMS PINAFORE
or The Lass That Loved a Sailor
1878
music by Arthur Sullivan
libretto by W.S. Gilbert

A Simple Sailor Lowly Born

from Act II

setting: England, the 19th century; quarterdeck of the *HMS Pinafore*, docked off Portsmouth
character: Josephine

Josephine's father is captain of the *HMS Pinafore*. Sir Joseph Porter, first Lord of the Admiralty, has proposed to Josephine, but she is deeply in love with Ralph Rackstraw, a lowly sailor. She wonders in this aria what she should do. There is something to be said for each of her suitors, and she weighs carefully the respective consequences of her actions.

HÉRODIADE
(Herodias)
1881
music by Jules Massenet
libretto by Paul Milliet, "Henri Grémont" (Georges Hartmann), and Angelo Zanardini (after the story by Gustave Flaubert)

Il est doux, il est bon

from Act I
setting: a courtyard in Herod's palace
character: Salomé

Phanuel, a Chaldean astrologer, sees Salomé enter the courtyard. He knows that she is the daughter of Queen Herodias, but she does not know this and is constantly in search of her real mother. In the course of this search she has fallen under the spell of John the Baptist, who is now a prisoner of Herod. She expresses her ardent infatuation for the prophet in this aria.

Celui dont la parole efface toutes peines,	*The one whose words erase all grief,*
le Prophète est ici! c'est vers lui que je vais!	*the Prophet is here! and it is he that I now seek!*
Il est doux, il est bon, sa parole est sereine:	*He is mild, he is good, his words are soothing:*
Il parle... tout se tait;	*He speaks... all is quiet;*
Plus léger sur la plaine	*Gently over the plain*
l'air attentif passe sans bruit;	*the wind listens without noise;*
il parle!	*he is speaking!*

Ah! quand reviendra-t-il? Quand pourrai-je l'entendre?	*Ah, when will he return? When will I hear him again?*
Je souffrais, j'étais seule et mon cœur s'est calmé	*I was suffering, I was alone but my heart grew calm*
En écoutant sa voix mélodieuse et tendre,	*Upon listening to his melodious and tender voice,*
mon cœur s'est calmé!	*my heart grew calm!*
Prophète bien aimé, puis-je vivre sans toi?	*Beloved Prophet, how can I live without you?*
C'est là! dans ce désert où la foule étonnée	*It was there! in the desert that the crowds*
avait suivi ses pas,	*followed him,*
qu'il m'accueillit un jour, enfant abandonnée!	*there that he welcomed me too one day, a forsaken child!*
et qu'il m'ouvrit ses bras!	*and opened his arms to me!*

MANON

1884
music by Jules Massenet
libretto by Henri Meilhac and Philippe Gille (after the novel *L'Histoire du Chevalier des Grieux et de Manon Lescaut* by Abbè Prévost)

Je suis encor

from Act I
setting: France, 1721; the courtyard of an inn at Amiens
character: Manon Lescaut

The devil-may-care Lescaut, a member of the Royal Guard, has been waiting for his young cousin, Manon, to arrive in a coach on the way to a convent school. When she appears she is even prettier and more naïve and charming than Lescaut had expected. She breathlessly relates the adventures of her journey.

Je suis encor tout étourdie…	*I'm still quite dazed;*
Je suis encor tout engourdie!	*I'm still quite numb!*
Ah! mon cousin! Excusez-moi!	*Ah, my cousin, excuse me!*
Excusez un moment d'émoi.	*Excuse an emotional moment.*
Je suis encor tout étourdie!	*I'm still quite numb!*
Pardonnez à mon bavardage.	*Pardon my chatter.*
J'en suis à mon premier voyage!	*I'm travelling for the first time!*
Le coche s'éloignait à peine,	*The coach had scarcely left*
que j'admirais de tous mes yeux	*when I was admiring – wide-eyed –*
les hameaux, les grands bois, la plaine,	*the hamlets, the forests, the plain,*
les voyageurs jeunes et vieux.	*the travellers young and old.*
Ah! mon cousin, excusez-moi!	*Ah, my cousin, excuse me!*
C'est mon premier voyage!	*This is my first trip!*
Je regardais fuir, curieuse,	*Curious, I watched fly by*
les arbres frissonnant au vent!	*the trees quivering in the wind!*
Et j'oubliais, toute joyeuse,	*And I forgot, full of joy,*
que je partais pour le couvent!	*that I was leaving for the convent!*
Devant tant de choses nouvelles,	*Faced with so many new things,*
ne riez pas, si je vous dis	*don't laugh if I tell you*
que je croyais avoir des ailes,	*that I thought I had wings*
et m'envoler en paradis!	*and was flying in paradise!*
Oui, mon cousin!	*Yes, my cousin!*
Puis, j'eus un moment de tristesse.	*Then I had a moment of sadness.*
Je pleurais, je ne sais pas quoi.	*I cried – I don't know why.*
L'instant d'après, je le confesse,	*A moment later, I confess,*
je riais, ah! ah! ah!	*I was laughing – ha! ha! ha! –*
mais sans savoir pourquoi!	*but without knowing why!*
Ah! mon cousin, excusez-moi.	*Ah, my cousin, excuse me.*
Ah! mon cousin, pardon!	*Ah, my cousin, pardon me!*
Je suis encor tout étourdie…	*I'm still quite dazed;*
Je suis encor tout engourdie!	*I'm still quite numb!*
Pardonnez à mon bavardage.	*Pardon my chatter.*
J'en suis à mon premier voyage!	*I'm travelling for the first time!*

Translation by Martha Gerhart

Obéissons quand leur voix appelle
(Gavotte)

from Act III, scene 1
setting: Paris, 1720s; the promenade of Cours la Reine
character: Manon Lescaut

Manon has become a great lady on the arm of the nobleman De Brétigny. Men and women gather about her as her name floats through the crowd, and she frivolously sings of the joys and satisfactions of her life. Then in the Gavotte she expresses her philosophy that love, laughter, and song must be enjoyed before the years weigh too heavily on a girl's shoulders.

Est-ce vrai? Grand merci!
Je consens, vu, que je suis bonne,
A laisser admirer ma charmante personne!

Je marche sur tous les chemins
aussi bien qu'une souveraine;
on s'incline, on baise mes mains,
car par la beauté je suis reine!

Mes chevaux courent à grands pas;
devant ma vie aventureuse,
les grands s'avancent chapeau bas;
je suis belle, je suis heureuse!

Autour de moi, tout doit fleurir!
Je vais à tout ce qui m'attire!
Et si Manon devait jamais mourir,
ce serait, mes amis, dans un éclat de rire!

Obéissons quand leur voix appelle
aux tendres amours, toujours, toujours, toujours
Tant que vous êtes belle,
usez sans les compter vos jours!

Profitons bien de la jeunesse,
de jours qu'amène le printemps;
aimons, rions, chantons sans cesse,
nous n'avons encore que vingt ans!
Ah! ah!

Le cœur, hélas, le plus fidèle,
Oublie en un jour l'amour,
Et la jeunesse ouvrant son aile
a disparu san retour!

Profitons bien de la jeunesse,
Bien court, hélas, est la printemps!
Aimons, chantons, rions sans cesse,
nous n'aurons pas toujours vingt ans!
Profitons bien de nos vingt ans!
Ah! ah!

Is that true? Many thanks!
I consent, considering, that I am good,
To admiring of my charming person!

I walk down every path
just like a sovereign,
people bow low, they kiss my hands,
because of my beauty I am a queen!

My horses run with great steps;
in front of my adventurous life,
grand men advance, hats raised;
I am beautiful, I am happy!

Around me, all must flower!
I go to everything that attracts me!
And if Manon ever were to die,
It would be, my friends, in a burst of laughter!

Obey when the voice calls
with tender love, always, always, always
As long as you are beautiful,
use your days without counting them!

Let us reap the benefits of youth,
of the days which springtime brings;
let us love, laugh, and sing unceasingly,
we're still only twenty years old!
Ha, ha!

The heart, alas, even the most loyal,
can forget love in one day,
and youth spreads its wings
and disappears, not to return!

Let us reap the benefits of youth,
Quite short, alas, is spring!
Let us love, sing, and laugh unceasingly,
we will not always be twenty years old!
Let us make the most of being twenty!
Ha, ha!

LA WALLY
1892
music by Alfredo Catalani
libretto by Luigi Illica (after *Die Geyer-Wally* by Wilhelmine von Hillern)

Ebben?... Ne andrò lontana

from Act I
setting: Austria, the Tyrol mountains, c. 1800, the village Hochstoff
character: Wally

Wally is the daughter of a rich landowner, Stromminger. Wally is attracted to a hunter from a nearby village, but her father will have none of such affection and insists that she marry Vincenzo Gellner, the steward of her father's estate. Wally stubbornly refuses and her father, in a fit of temper, banishes her, slamming the door of the cottage as he goes in. She vows to wander alone and friendless into the mountains.

Ebben?... Ne andrò lontana,	*Well?... I'll go far from here,*
come va l'eco della pia campana...	*like the distant echo of the church bell...*
là, fra la neve bianca!...	*there, in the white snow!...*
là, fra le nubi d'or!...	*there, in the clouds of gold!...*
laddove la speranza	*there is where hope*
è rimpianto, è dolor!	*is regret, is pain!*
O della madre mia casa gioconda,	*Oh, merry house of my mother,*
la Wally ne andrà da te lontana assai,	*Wally will leave you, journeying far from you,*
e forse a te non farà mai più ritorno,	*maybe to you she'll not return,*
né più la rivedrai!	*never will you see her again!*
Mai più, mai più!	*Never, never!*
Ne andrò sola e lontana,	*I'll go by myself and far from here,*
come l'eco della pia campana...	*like the distant echo of the church bell...*
là, fra la neve bianca;	*there, in the white snow;*
ne andrò sola e lontana	*I'll go by myself and far from here*
e fra le nubi d'or!	*there in the clouds of gold!*
Ma fermo il piè'! Ne andiam,	*But my foot is heavy! We must go,*
che lunga è la via! Ne andiam!	*so long is the journey! We must go!*

WERTHER

1892
music by Jules Massenet
libretto by Edouard Blau, Georges Hartmann and Paul Milliet (after the novel *Die Leiden des jungen Werther* by Johann Wolfgang von Goethe)

Frère! voyez!... Du gai soleil

from Act II
setting: the small town of Wetzlar near Frankfurt, September, 1780s; the village green; a sunny Sunday afternoon
character: Sophie

The poet Werther is desperately in love with Charlotte, who is married to Albert. It is the celebration for the pastor's golden wedding aniversary. Sophie, Charlotte's sister, reflects the joy of the day, carrying flowers for the pastor and stopping to ask the always-somewhat-disconsolate Werther for the first minuet of the afternoon.

Frère! voyez!... Voyez le beau bouquet!	*Brother, look!... Look at the beautiful bouquet!*
J'ai mis, pour le Pasteur, le jardin au pillage!	*I pilfered the garden for it, for the Pastor!*
Et puis, l'on va danser!	*And then, everyone is going to dance!*
Pour le premier menuet c'est sur vous que je compte.	*I'm counting on you for the first minuet.*
Ah! le sombre visage!	*Ah, your gloomy countenance!*
Mais aujour-d'hui, monsieur Werther,	*But today, monsieur Werther,*
tout le monde est joyeux!	*the whole world is joyful!*
Le bonheur est dans l'air!	*Happiness is in the air!*
Du gai soleil, plein de flamme	*From the bright sunshine, all ablaze*
dans l'azur resplendissant	*in the resplendent blue sky,*
la pure clarté descend de nos fronts	*the pure light descends from our heads*
jusqu'à notre âme!	*to our souls!*
Tout le monde est joyeux!	*The whole world is joyful!*
Le bonheur est dans l'air!	*Happiness is in the air!*
Et l'oiseau qui monte aux cieux	*And the bird which soars to the heavens*
dans la brise qui soupire	*in the breeze which sighs*
est revenu pour nous dire	*has returned to tell us*
que Dieu permet d'être heureux!	*that God allows us to be happy!*
Tout le monde est joyeux!	*The whole world is joyful!*
Le bonheur est dans l'air!	*Happiness is in the air!*
Tout le monde est heureux!	*The whole world is happy!*

Translation by Martha Gerhart

MANON LESCAUT

1893
music by Giacomo Puccini
libretto by Marco Praga, Domenico, Luigi Illica, Giuseppe Giacosa, Giulio Ricordi, and the composer (after the novel by Abbè Prévost)

In quelle trine morbide

from Act II
setting: Paris, 1720s; the elegant home of Geronte de Ravoir, an elderly Parisian gallant who is the courtesan Manon's lover
character: Manon Lescaut

Lescaut, Manon's cousin, wanders into the splendor of her boudoir and compliments himself on having helped her to find a rich lover to satisfy her ambition. She answers that all of this luxury can't replace the real love that she felt for her Des Grieux.

In quelle trine morbide
nell'alcova dorata v'è un silenzio,
un gelido mortal, v'è un silenzio,
un freddo che m'agghiaccia!
Ed io che m'ero avvezza
a una carezza voluttuosa
di labbra ardenti e d'infuocate braccia
or ho tutt'altra cosa!

O mia dimora umile,
tu mi ritorni innanzi
gaia, isolata, bianca
come un sogno gentile
di pace e d'amor!

In that delicate lace
in the gilded alcove there is a silence,
a deathly chill, a silence,
A chill that horrifies me!
And I, who became accustomed
to a seductive caress
of ardent lips and blazing arms
now I have something very different!

O my humble dwelling,
you return to me
merry, alone, white
like a gentle dream
of peace and love!

THAÏS

1894
music by Jules Massenet
libretto by Louis Gallet (after the novel by Anatole France)

Dis-moi que je suis belle

from Act II, scene 1
setting: Alexandria, the 4th century; the residence of Thaïs
character: Thaïs

Thaïs, actress and courtesan, has been surrounded by companions and revelers. She dismisses them and gives voice to her world-weariness, musing on the shallowness of her existence. Gazing into a mirror and sensing that her beauty is her only real treasure, she prays to Venus that it will last her until the end of time.

Ah! je suis seule, seule, enfin!
Tous ces hommes
ne sont qu'indifférence et que brutalité.
Les femmes sont méchantes...
et les heures pesantes!
J'ai l'âme vide... Où trouver le repos?
Et comment fixer le bonheur?
Ô mon miroir fidèle, rassure-moi!

Ah! I am alone, alone, finally!
All these men
are only indifference and brutality.
The women are wicked...
and the hours heavy!
My being is empty... Where to find repose?
And how to achieve contentment?
O my loyal mirror, reassure me!

Dis-moi que je suis belle	*Tell me that I am beautiful*
et que je serai belle éternellement!	*and that I will be beautiful forever!*
Éternellement!	*Forever!*
Que rien ne flétrira les roses	*That nothing will wilt the roses*
de mes lèvres,	*of my lips,*
que rien ne ternira l'or pur	*that nothing will tarnish the pure gold*
de mes cheveux!	*of my hair!*
Dis-le moi! Dis-le moi!	*Tell me! Tell me!*
Dis-moi que je suis belle	*Tell me that I am beautiful*
et que je serai belle éternellement!	*and that I will be beautiful forever!*
Éternellement!	*Forever!*
Ah! je serai belle éternellement!	*Ah! I will be beautiful forever!*
Ah! Tais-toi, voix impitoyable,	*Ah! Quiet, unpitying voice,*
voix qui me dis:	*voice that tells me:*
Thaïs, tu vieilliras!	*Thaïs, you will age!*
Thaïs, tu vieilliras!	*Thaïs, you will age!*
Un jour, ainsi, Thaïs ne serait plus Thaïs!	*Then, one day, Thaïs would no longer be Thaïs!*
Non! Non! je n'y puis croire!	*No, no! I will not accept it!*
Toi, Vénus, réponds-moi de ma beauté!	*You, Venus, respond to me about my beauty!*
Vénus, réponds-moi de son éternité!	*Venus, respond to me about its eternity!*
Vénus, invisible et présente!	*Venus, invisible and present!*
Vénus, enchantement de l'ombre!	*Venus, enchantment of the shadow!*
Vénus! Réponds-moi! Réponds-moi!	*Venus! Respond! Respond!*
Dis-moi que je suis belle	*Tell me that I am beautiful*
et que je serai belle éternellement!	*and that I will be beautiful forever!*
Éternellement!	*Forever!*
Que rien ne flétrira les roses	*That nothing will wilt the roses*
de mes lèvres,	*of my lips,*
que rien ne ternira l'or pur	*that nothing will tarnish the pure gold*
de mes cheveux!	*of my hair!*
Dis-le moi! Dis-le moi!	*Tell me! Tell me!*
Dis-moi que je suis belle	*Tell me that I am beautiful*
et que je serai belle éternellement!	*and that I will be beautiful forever!*
Éternellement!	*Forever!*
Ah! je serai belle éternellement!	*Ah! I will be beautiful forever!*

LOUISE

1900
music and libretto by Gustave Charpentier

Depuis le jour

from Act III, scene 1
setting: Paris, c. 1900; a small garden on the side of a hill in Montmartre
character: Louise

Julien, a poet, has finally succeeded in taking the seamstress Louise from her parents and bringing her to his cottage in Montmartre. It is twilight and the two young lovers are sitting on their porch with the glowing vista of Paris before them. Louise looks at Julien and tries to express the almost unutterable joy she feels in this new life with her lover.

Depuis le jour où je me suis donnée,	*Since the day I gave myself,*
toute fleurie semble ma destinée.	*my destiny seems to be flowering.*
Je crois rêver sous un ciel de féerie,	*I seem to be slumbering beneath a fairyland,*
l'âme encore grisée	*my heart still enchanted*
de ton premier baiser!	*by that first kiss!*
Quelle belle vie!	*What a beautiful life!*
Mon rêve n'était pas un rêve!	*My dream was not a dream!*
Ah! je suis heureuse!	*Oh! I am so lucky!*
L'amour étend sur moi ses ailes!	*Love extends its wings over me!*

Au jardin de mon cœur	*In the garden of my heart*
chante une joie nouvelle!	*sings a new joy!*
Tout vibre,	*Everything reverberates,*
tout se réjouit de mon triomphe!	*everything rejoices in my triumph!*
Autour de moi tout est sourire,	*All is smiles around me,*
lumière et joie!	*light and joy!*
Et je tremble délicieusement	*And I tremble deliciously*
au souvenir charmant	*at the rapturous memory*
du premier jour d'amour!	*of the first day of love!*
Quelle belle vie!	*What a beautiful life!*
Ah! je suis heureuse! trop heureuse...	*Oh, how lucky I am! too lucky...*
Et je tremble délicieusement	*And I tremble deliciously*
au souvenir charmant	*at the rapturous memory*
du premier jour d'amour!	*of the first day of love!*

RUSALKA

1901
music by Antonín Dvořák
libretto by Jaroslav Kvapil (after Freidrich Heinrich Karl de la Motte Fouqué's novel *Undine*, with additions from Hans Christian Andersen's story *The Little Mermaid* and ideas from Gerhart Hauptmann's play *The Sunken Bell*)

Měsíčku na nebi hlubokém
(Song to the Moon)

from Act I
setting: fairytale Europe; a meadow clearing in the woods, on the edge of a lake
character: Rusalka

Rusalka is a water nymph who has just confessed to Vodník, a water gnome, that she has fallen in love with a human, a Prince, whom she has seen swimming in the lake. Vodník is horrified and sinks back into the water, telling her as he disappears that she must seek help from Ježibaba, a witch. First, Rusalka turns to the moon and urges it to tell the man she loves that she waits for him.

Měsíčku na nebi hlubokém,	*Moon in the broad sky,*
světlo tvé daleko vidí,	*your beams see afar,*
po světě bloudíš širokém,	*around the entire Earth you roam,*
díváš se v příbytky lidí,	*you see into the homes of people,*
po světě bloudíš širokém,	*around the entire Earth you roam,*
díváš se v příbytky lidí.	*you see into the homes of people.*
Měsíčku, postůj chvíli, řekni mi,	*Moon, pause for a moment, answer me,*
kde je můj milý,	*where is my love,*
měsíčku, postůj chvíli, řekni mi, řekni,	*moon, pause for a moment, answer me, answer,*
kde je můj milý?	*where is my love?*
Řekni mu, stříbrný měsíčku,	*Tell him, oh pale moon,*
mé že jej objímá rámě,	*that my arms envelop him,*
aby si alespoň chviličku	*so that he, for at least a moment,*
vzpomenul ve snění na mne,	*might see me in his dreams,*
aby si alespoň chviličku	*so that he, for at least a moment,*
vzpomenul ve snění na mne.	*might see me in his dreams.*
Zasvěť' mu do daleka, zasvěť' mu, řekni mu,	*Give him your beams afar, give him your beams, tell him,*
řekni, kdo tu naň čeká;	*tell, that I wait for him here;*
zasvěť' mu do daleka, zasvěť' mu, řekni mu,	*give him your beams afar, give him your beams, tell him,*
řekni, kdo tu naň čeká!	*tell, that I wait for him here!*
O mně-li duše lidská sní,	*Oh, if his human heart dreams of me,*
ať' se tou vzpomínkou vzbudí!	*let this vision awaken!*
Měsíčku, nezhasni, nezhasni,	*Moon, stay with me, stay with me,*
měsíčku, nezhasni!	*oh, moon, stay with me!*

DIE LUSTIGE WITWE
(The Merry Widow)
1905
music by Franz Lehár
libretto by Viktor Leon and Leo Stein

Es lebt' eine Vilja
(Vilia)

from Act II
setting: Paris, *c*1900; the garden of Madame Glawari's mansion; late afternoon
character: Hanna Glawari

Hanna, a young widow of the wealthiest man in Pontevedro, is giving a party in her palace. Members of the Pontevedrian Embassy and their wives and French aristocrats are guests. She entertains with dancers in native costume and then tells a traditional national folk tale in song.

Nun lasst uns aber wie daheim jetzt singen unsern Ringelreim von einer Fee, die wie bekannt, daheim die Vilja wird genannt!	But let us now, as in our homeland, sing our refrain about a sprite who, as is well-known in our homeland, is called Vilia.
Es lebt' eine Vilja, ein Waldmägdelein, ein Jäger erschaut' sie im Felsengestein! Dem Burschen, dem wurde so eigen zu Sinn, er schaute und schaut' auf das Waldmägdlein hin. Und ein nie gekannter Schauer fasst' den jungen Jägersmann, sehnsuchtsvoll fing er still zu seufzen an!	There once lived a Vilia, a wood-maiden. a hunter noticed her on the rocky cliffs. The fellow, to whom it felt very strange, looked up and gazed upon the wood-maiden. And a thrill never known to him before seized the young huntsman; full of longing, he began to sigh softly!
Vilja, o Vilja, du Waldmägdelein, fass' mich und lass' mich dein Trautliebster sein. Vilja, o Vilja, was thust du mir an? Band fleht ein liebkranker Mann!	Vilia, oh Vilia, you wood-maiden, captivate me and let me be your dearest love. Vilia, oh Vilia, what are you doing to me? Anxiously implores a lovesick man!
Das Waldmägdlein streckte die Hand nach ihm aus und zog ihn hinein in ihr felsiges Haus. Dem Burschen die Sinne vergangen fast sind, so liebt und so küsst gar kein irdisches Kind.	The wood-maiden extended her hand to him and drew him into her rocky dwelling. The fellow's senses almost expired, as no earthly child ever loved and kissed so.
Als sie sich dann satt geküsst verschwand sie zu der selben Frist! Einmal noch hat der Arme sie gegrüsst:	Then, when they were satiated with kissing, she disappeared at the very moment. Once more, the poor man greeted her:
Vilja, o Vilja, usw.	Vilia, oh Vilia, etc.

Translation by Martha Gerhart

LA RONDINE
(The Swallow)
1917
music by Giacomo Puccini
libretto by Giuseppe Adami (after a German libretto by Alfred Willner and Heinz Reichert)

Chi il bel sogno di Doretta
(La Canzone di Doretta)

from Act I
setting: Paris, the Second Empire of Napoleon III, 1850s; an elegant salon in Magda de Civry's home
character: Magda de Civry

Prunier, a poet, is entertaining a sophisticated salon audience, explaining the concept of sentimental love that is all the rage in Paris. No one except Magda takes very seriously his verses about his heroine Doretta who spurns a king's treasures for real love. He eloquently recites and sings them at the piano but suddenly has a lapse, and Magda volunteers to complete his thoughts. She repeats his inventions with her own twist and adds an especially exquisite ending.

Chi il bel sogno di Doretta potè indovinar?	*Who could guess Doretta's beautiful dream?*
Il suo mister come mai finì?	*How did its mystery end?*
Ahimè! un giorno uno studente	*Alas, one day a student*
in bocca la baciò,	*kissed her lips,*
e fu quel bacio rivelazione:	*and that kiss was revelation:*
Fu la passione!	*It was passion!*
Folle amore! Folle ebbrezza!	*Frenzied love! Frenzied rapture!*
Chi la sottil carezza	*Who could ever describe*
d'un bacio così ardente	*the subtle caress of a*
mai ridir potrà?	*kiss so ardent?*
Ah! mio sogno! Ah! mia vita!	*Ah, my dream! Ah, my life!*
Che importa la ricchezza	*Of what importance is wealth*
se alfin è rifiorita la felicità!	*if, at last, happiness has blossomed again!*
O sogno d'or poter amar così!	*Oh golden dream, to be able to love like that!*

Translation by Martha Gerhart

SUOR ANGELICA

(Sister Angelica)
(the second one-act opera from *Il Trittico*)
1918
music by Giacomo Puccini
libretto by Giovacchino Forzano

Senza mamma

in one act

setting: near Siena, Italy, 17th century; a convent
character: Suor Angelica

Angelica came to the convent seven years ago and has had no visitors. Her aunt the Principessa has at last come and, in their interview, Angelica inquires about the baby boy she was forced to leave behind. Her aunt tells her he died of a fever. Angelica is overcome with grief, but the Principessa insists she sign the papers that she brought, whereby the nun renounces her birthright. When left alone, Angelica mourns her lost child but knows that he is with God in heaven.

Senza mamma, o bimbo,	*Without your mother, o babe,*
tu sei morto!	*you died!*
Le tue labbra, senza i baci miei,	*Your lips, without my kisses,*
scoloriron fredde, fredde!	*grew pale and chilled, chilled!*
E chiudesti,	*And you closed,*
o bimbo, gli occhi belli!	*O babe, your beautiful eyes!*
Non potendo carezzarmi,	*Powerless to caress me,*
le manine componesti in croce!	*you crossed your little hands!*
E tu sei morto	*And you died*
senza sapere	*never knowing*
quanto t'amava	*how much you were loved*
questa tua mamma!	*by your mother!*

Ora che sei un angelo del cielo,
ora tu puoi vederla la tua mamma!
Tu puoi scendere giù pel firmamento
ed aleggiare intorno a me... ti sento...
Sei qui... sei qui...
mi baci e m'accarezzi.
Ah! dimmi, quando in ciel potrò vederti?
Quando potrò baciarti?...
O dolce fine d'ogni mio dolore,
quando in cielo con te potrò salire?...
Quando potrò morire?
Dillo alla mamma, creatura bella,
con un leggero scintillar di stella...
parlami, amore, amore!

Now that you are an angel in heaven,
finally you can see your mother!
You may descend to earth
and hover near me... I feel you...
You are here... you are here...
you kiss me and you caress me.
Ah! tell me, when will I see you in heaven?
When will I kiss you?...
O beloved end of all my pain,
when will I be with you in heaven?
When will I die?
Tell your mother, beautiful creature,
with the twinkle of a star...
speak to me, my love, my love!

DIE TOTE STADT
(The Dead City)
1920
music by Erich Wolfgang Korngold
libretto by "Paul Schott" (actually the composer and his father, Julius Korngold)

Glück, das mir verblieb
(Marietta's Lied)

from Act I

setting: Bruges, late 19th century
character: Marietta

Paul is inconsolable over the death of his young wife Marie, but then he meets a woman who looks much like her and he invites her to his home. This Marietta is a dancer, uninhibited and beautiful. He wraps her in a shawl of his Marie's and takes a lute from the wall and hands it to her. She thinks he must be a painter looking for a subject, but says that an old lute demands an old song and sings for him.

Glück, das mir verblieb,
rück zu mir, mein treues Lieb.
Abend sinkt im Hag
bist mir Licht und Tag.
Bange pochet Herz an Herz
Hoffnung schwingt sich himmelwärts.

Good fortune, remaining near to me,
Come to me, my true love.
Evening sinks into the grove
You are my light and day.
Timidly beats heart on heart
Hope rises toward heaven.

Wie wahr, ein traurig Lied.
Das Lied vom treuen Lieb,
das sterben muß.
Ich kenne das Lied.
Ich hört es oft in jungen,
in schöneren Tagen.
Es hat noch eine Strophe
weiß ich sie noch?

So true, a mournful song.
The song of true love,
that must die.
I know this song.
I heard it oftentimes in younger,
in fairer days.
It still has one more verse
do I know it still?

Naht auch Sorge trüb,
rück zu mir, mein treues Lieb.
Neig dein blaß Gesicht
Sterben trennt uns nicht.
Mußt du einmal von mir gehn,
glaub, es gibt ein Auferstehn.

Though grief becomes clouded,
Come to me, my true love.
Lean to me your pale face
Death will not part us.
If you must one day part from me,
Believe, there is rebirth.

THE BALLAD OF BABY DOE
1956
music by Douglas Moore
libretto by John Latouche (based on the life of Elizabeth "Baby" Doe Tabor, 1854-1935)

Dearest Mama

from Act I, scene 4
setting: Leadville, Colorado, 1880; the lobby of the Clarendon Hotel
character: Elizabeth "Baby" Doe Tabor

When Baby Doe Tabor divorced Harvey Doe and moved from Central City to Leadville, Colorado, she met the famous silver tycoon Horace Tabor. The two were immediately attracted to each other. Baby knows that the gossips are talking and that there will be trouble with Horace's domineering wife Augusta before long, so she packs her bags and is planning to leave Leadville. She shares her feelings in a letter to her mother, which she pens in the lobby of the Clarendon Hotel. The epic story of the opera is based on a true segment of Americana.

A STREETCAR NAMED DESIRE
1998
music by André Previn
libretto by Philip Littell (based on the play by Tennessee Williams)

I want magic!

from Act III, scene 2
setting: the Elysian Fields section of New Orleans, the present (1947); a bedroom in the apartment of Stanley and Stella Kowalski
character: Blanche DuBois

Blanche DuBois comes to New Orleans to visit her sister Stella after her world comes tumbling down around her, and she loses her ancestral home and her job. Stella's husband Stanley is an ex-GI truck driver, and he takes great exception to Blanche's sophisticated airs. He knows that she is consuming a great deal of liquor and has serious misgivings about who and what she really is. Stanley has introduced her to his friend Mitch, and they've hit it off rather well, but when Stanley substantiates his suspicions about Blanche's unsavory reputation he shares his findings with Mitch. Mitch visits Blanche, crestfallen and drunk, and tries to turn the lights on in the dimly lit room, because it occurs to him he's never seen the woman in the light of day. She struggles to turn them off again saying that magic is more important in life than reality.

Non disperar
from
GIULIO CESARE

George Frideric Handel

CLEOPATRA: *(in a rage)*

An - zi tu pur, ef - fe - mi - na - to'a - man - te,   va' dell' e -

tà sui pri - mi na - ti al - bo - ri, di re-gno in - ve - ce a col - ti - var gli a -

Allegro ma non troppo

mo - ri!

* appoggiatura recommended
realization by Richard Walters

Non di-spe - rar, non di-spe - rar; chi sa? se al re - gno_ non l'a - vrai,_____ a - vrai sor-te in a - mor,_____

se al re-gno non l'a-vrai, a-

vrai sor-te in a-mor, a-vrai ___ sor-te in a-mor; chi sa? chi

sa?

Non di-spe-rar, chi sa? se al

[f]

[mf]

re-gno non l'a vrai, a-vrai sor-te in a-mor, ___

Piangerò la sorte mia
from
GIULIO CESARE

George Frideric Handel

CLEOPATRA:

E pur co - sì [in] un gior-no per-do fa - sti e gran - dez-ze? Ahi, fa - to

ri - o! Ce - sa-re, il mio bel nu-me, è for-se e-stin-to; Cor-

ne - lia e Se - sto in-er-mi son, nè san-no dar-mi soc - cor-so. Oh Di - o!

Non res - ta al-cu-na spe-me al vi - ver mi - o.

* appoggiatura recommended
realization by Richard Walters

Pian - ge - rò, pian - ge - rò la __ sor - te

mi - a, sì cru - de - le __ e tan - to

ri - a, fin - ché vi - ta in pet - to a - vrò.

Pian - ge - rò, __ pian - ge - rò la

sor - te mi - a, sì cru - de - le e tan - to

ri - a, pian - ge - rò la sor - te mi - a, sì cru - de - le _____ e tan - to

ri - a, _____ fin - ché vi - ta _____ in pet - to a -

vrò, fin - ché vi - ta, fin - ché vi -

ta in pet - to a - vrò.

Fine

Allegro [*mf*]

Ma poi mor - ta d'o - gn'in-tor - no

[*mf*]

il ti - ran - no e not - te e gior - no

fat - ta spet - tro a - gi - te - rò,

fat - ta spet -

- tro, fat - ta spet - tro a - gi - te - rò.

Ma poi mor - ta

Stizzoso, mio stizzoso

from
LA SERVA PADRONA

Giovanni Battista Pergolesi

so - gna al mio di - vie-to star che - to, che - to, e

non par - la - re! Zit! Zit! Ser - pi - na__ vuol co -

sì. Voi fa - te il bo - ri - o - so, ma non vi può gio - va - re! Bi - so-gna al mio di -

vie - to star che-to, e non par - la - re! Zit! Zit! Che -

D.S. al Fine

Lo temei… Lo potrò! Ma frattanto, oh infelice

from
PARIDE ED ELENA

Christoph Willibald von Gluck

Lo te-mei: non mi sen-to in fac-cia a lui va-lor che ba-sti. Ap-

pe - na fre-nar-mi sep-pi. E - ro ri-dot-ta al pun - to d'a - prir-gli, di sve-lar-gli

tut - ta l'a - ni-ma mi - a. Ah, la pos-sie-de, vi re-gna, n'è ti-ran-no; e lo co-

* appoggiatura recommended

Moderato

Ho già de - ci - so!

Lo po -

Andante

trò! Ma frat - tan - to, oh in - fe -

li - ce, o - dio ed a - mo, ri -

sol - vo e mi pen - to; pie - tà,

sde-gno, ti-mo-re, con-ten-to a vi-cen-da mi fan-no pe-

nar, a vi-cen-da mi fan-no pe-nar, mi

Moderato

fan-no pe-nar. Co-sì

breve
Andante

vo-glio! Sì, men-tre è lon-ta-no, il ti-ran-no che i cep-pi me

die - de;   ma   se   pre - ga,   se   pian - ge al mio

p assai

pie - de,   non   so   più   che   ta - ce - re e tre - mar,

ma   se   pre - ga,   se   pian - ge al mio pie - de,   non   so

più   che   ta - ce - re e tre - mar,   che   ta - ce - re

fin - go, co' suoi mo - ti mi

vie - ne a tur - bar! Oh in - fe -

li - ce, o - dio ed a - mo, ri - sol - vo e mi

pen - to, ri - sol - vo e mi pen - to; ma il mio

bar,   quel che pen - so, che so - gno, che

fin - go   co' suoi mo - ti mi vie - ne a tur -

bar, _____ co' suoi mo - ti mi

vie - ne a tur - bar, _ co' suoi mo - ti mi

Qual vita è questa mai... Che fiero momento

from
ORFEO ED EURIDICE

Christoph Willibald von Gluck

min - cio!   E qual ar - can m'as-con-de Or-feo?

Trat - to m'av-ria   dal re - ces - so fe - ral   per far-si reo   del per - fi-do ab-ban

do - no? Si smen - ti - sce la lu - ce, o ciel, ag-li oc - chi mie - i.

Allegro moderato

Op-pres-so in se - no mi di - ven - ta af - fan - no - so il re - spi-rar.

pp

Tre-mo... va - cil -lo... e sen - to

p

fra l'an - go - scia e il ter - ro - re,

* appoggiatura recommended

quan - do al-l'eb-brez - za, re - di - vi - va, a -

spi - ro, da un pal - pi - to cru -

del sen - to, ahi - mè! vib-rar-mi il cor.

Aria
Allegro

Che fie - ro mo - men - to! Che bar - ba - ra

sor - te! Pas - sar _ dal - la mor - te a tan - to do - lor! _ Che

Lento

Allegro

fie - ro mo - men - to! Che bar - ba - ra

sor - te! Pas - sar dal - la mor - te a

tan - to do - lor! Pas - sar dal - la mor - te a

tan - to do - lor, a

* optional ending

bar - ba - ra sor - te! Pas - sar dal la

mor - te a tan - to do - lor, pas -

sar dal la mor - te a tan -

- to do - lor, a tan -

to do - lor!

Zeffiretti lusinghieri

from
IDOMENEO

Wolfgang Amadeus Mozart

* Appoggiatura recommended
recitative is optional

Zef - fi - ret - ti lu - sin - ghie - ri, deh vo - la -

te al mio te - so - ro: e gli di - te,

ch'io l'a - do - ro, che mi ser - bi il cor ____ fe - del.

Zef - fi - ret - ti lu - sin - ghie - ri, deh vo - la - te al mio te -

so - ro: e gli di - te, ch'io l'a - do - ro,   che mi

serbi il cor ___ fedel, che mi serbi il

cor ___ fedel, ___ il cor ___ fe-

del, ___ il cor ___ fedel.

E voi

ciel. _____ Zef - fi - ret - ti lu - sin - ghie - ri,

deh vo - la - - -

- - - te al mio te -

so - ro: e gli di - te, ch'io l'a-

do - ro, che_mi_ser - bi il cor ___ fe - del.

fp

Zef - fi - ret - ti lu - sin - ghie - ri, deh vo - la - te al mio te -

mfp *simile* *mfp*

so - ro: e gli di - te, ch'io l'a - do - ro,

che mi ser - bi il cor ___ fe - del,

mfp *sfp*

che mi ser - bi il cor ____ fe - del, ____

il cor ____ fe - del, ____

il cor ____ fe - del.

Ach, ich liebte, war so glücklich
from
DIE ENTFÜHRUNG AUS DEM SERAIL

Wolfgang Amadeus Mozart

hin mein gan-zes Herz, gab da - hin _____ mein _ gan - zes

Herz.

Allegro

Doch wie schnell _ schwand _ mei - ne

Freu - de, doch wie schnell _ schwand _ mei - ne Freu - de!

Tren - nung _ war mein _ ban - ges _ Los, und nun

76

In uomini, in soldati
from
COSÌ FAN TUTTE

Wolfgang Amadeus Mozart

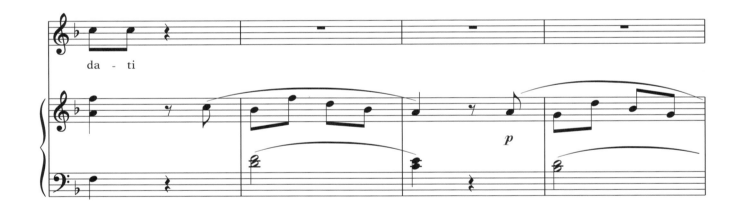

uo - mi - ni spe - ra - re fe - del - tà? In sol -

da - ti __ spe - ra - re fe - del - tà, fe - del - tà, fe - del -

(laughing)

tà? Non vi fa - te sen - tir, per ca - ri - tà! Non vi fa - te sen - tir, per ca - ri -

Allegretto

tà! Di pa - sta si - mi - le son tut - ti quan - ti, son tut - ti

quan - ti, le fron-de mo - bi-li l'au-re in-co - stan - ti han più de - gli uo - mi - ni sta - bi - li -

tà. Men-ti - te la - gri-me, fal - la - ci sguar - di,

vo-ci in-gan - ne - vo-li, vez - zi bu - giar - di son le pri - ma - rie ___

___ lor qua - li - tà, son le pri - ma - rie ___ lor qua - li -

tà. In noi non a - ma-no che il lor di - let - to; poi ci di-spre-gia-no, ne - gan-ci af-

fet - to, nè val da' bar - ba-ri chie-der pie - tà, nè val da' bar - ba-ri chie-der pie -

tà, chie - der pie - tà, chie - der pie -

tà. Pa-ghiam, o fem - mi-ne d'u-gual mo -

a-miam per co-mo-do, per va-ni - tà, la ra la, la ra la, la ra la

la, a-miam per co-mo-do, per va-ni - tà, _____ a-miam per co-mo-do, per va-ni -

tà, _____ a-miam per co-mo-do, per va-ni - tà.

Una donna a quindici anni
from
COSÌ FAN TUTTE

Wolfgang Amadeus Mozart

mo - ra - no gli a - man - ti, fin-ger ri - so, fin-ger pian - ti, in-ven-

tar i bei per-chè, fin-ger ri - so, fin-ger pian - ti, in-ven-

Allegretto

tar i bei per-chè. Dee in un mo-

men - to dar ret-ta a cen - to, col-le pu-pil - le par-lar con mil - le,

dar spe - me a tut - ti, sien bel-li o brut - ti, sa - per na -

scon - der-si sen - za con - fon - der-si, sen - za ar - ros - si - re sa - per men -

ti - re, sa - per men - ti - re, e qual re - gi - na dall' al - to so - glio col "pos-so e

vo - glio" far-si ub - bi - dir, e qual re -

gi - na col "pos - so e vo - glio" far - si ub - bi - dir.

Par ch'ab-bian gu - sto di tal dot-tri - na; vi - va De -

spi - na, che sa ser - vir, _____ che sa ser - vir.

Dee in un mo - men - to dar ret-ta a cen - to, col-le pu -

dir, _____ sì, _____ far - si ub - bi - dir.

Par ch'ab-bian gu - sto di tal dot-tri - na; vi - va De -

spi - na, che sa ser - vir, vi - va De-spi - na, che sa ser - vir, vi - va De-

spi - na, che sa ser - vir, _____ che sa ser - vir, _____ che sa ser - vir.

S'altro che lacrime

from
LA CLEMENZA DI TITO

Wolfgang Amadeus Mozart

Tempo di Minuetto

SERVILIA:

S'al - tro che la - cri - me per _ lui non _ ten - ti, tut - to il tuo pian - ge-re non - gio - ve - rà, tut - to il tu - o pian - ge-re non - gio - ve - rà, non gio - ve - rà.

A __ que - sta in-u -ti-le pie - tà _____ che sen - ti,

oh _ quan - to è si - mi-le la cru - del - tà, la ____

cru - del - tà. S'al - tro che la -cri-me per lui non _

ten - ti, tut - to il tuo pian - ge-re _____ non _ gio - ve -

rà, _____ tut - to il tu - o pian - ge-re, tut - to il tu - o

pian - ge-re non gio - ve - rà, _____ non gio - ve -

rà, _____ non gio - ve - rà.

Einst träumte meiner sel'gen Base...
Trübe Augen
from
DER FREISCHÜTZ

Carl Maria von Weber

Au - gen wie Feu-er, mit klir - ren-der _ Ket - te. Es nah - te _ dem _

Bet - te, in welch - em sie schlief— ich mei-ne die Ba - se mit krei-di-ger

Na - se— und stöhn - te, ach! so hohl, und ächz - te, ach! so tief! Sie

kreuz - te sich, rief, nach man-chem Angst- und Stoß - ge - bet: Su - san - ne!

tau - gen __ ei - nem __ hol - den __ Bräut - chen __ nicht.

Trü - be Au - gen, Lieb - chen, __ tau - gen nicht, _____

trü - be Au - gen, Lieb - chen, tau - gen ei - nem

hol - den __ Bräut - - - -

- chen nicht.

Daß ____ durch Bli - cke

sie _____ er - qui - cke   und __ be - glü - cke,

- ste Pflicht.

Lass in ö - den Mau - ern

Bü - ße - rin - nen trau - ern; dir _____ winkt _

ros'- ger Hoff - nung_ Licht! _ Schon ent - zün - det _ sind_ die_

Ker - zen _ zum_ Ver - ein _ ge - treu - er _ Her - zen;

schon ent - zün - det sind _ die _ Ker - zen, _

dir _ winkt ros' - ger Hoff - nung Licht. _ Hol - de _

hol - de Freun - din, hol - de,

za - ge nicht, hol - de

Freun - din, hol - de Freun - din,

za - - - - - - ge

Oh! quante volte

from

I CAPULETI E I MONTECCHI

Vincenzo Bellini

Andante maestoso

* Introduction may begin here.

Tempo I

ra - li.

Ar - do... u - na vam - pa, un fo - co

tut - ta mi strug - ge.

Un re-fri-ge-rio ai ven - ti io chie-do in - va - no!

O - ve sei tu, Ro-me-o? In qual ter - ra t'ag-gi - ri?

Do-ve, do - ve in-vi - ar-ti, do-ve   i miei so - spi -

ri? ___

Andante sostenuto

qua - le ar - dor t'at - ten - do, e in-gan - no il mio, il mio de-

sir!

Rag - gio del tuo sem - bian - te, ah! par-mi il bril-lar del

gior - no: ah! l'au - ra che spi - ra in - tor - no

mi sem- bra un tuo so - spir, ah! l'au - ra che spi - ra in-

tor - no mi sem- bra un tu -

col canto

a piacere

- o, un tuo so - spir.

p

pp

Ah! forse è lui... Sempre libera

from
LA TRAVIATA

Giuseppe Verdi

gio - ia ch'io non co-nob-bi, es-ser a-ma - ta a-man-do! E sde-

gnar-la pos-s'i-o per l'a-ri-de fol-li-e del vi-ver mi -

Andantino

o?

Ah! for - se è lui che l'a-ni-ma so-lin-ga ne' tu - mul - ti,

so-lin-ga ne' tu - mul - ti, go - dea so - ven - te pin - ge -

re de' suoi co-lo - ri oc - cul - ti, de' suoi co-lo - ri oc - cul - ti!

Lui che mo-de - sto e vi - gi - le al-l'e-gre so - glie a - sce - se,

e nuo-va feb-bre ac - ce - se de-stan-do-mi al - l'a - mor.

li - zia,   de-li zia al-cor!   ah, _____ de - li - zia al

Allegro (♩ = 120)

cor!   Fol - li - e!   Fol - li - e!

De - li - rio va - no è que-sto!...   Po - ve - ra

don - na!   so - la!   ab - ban - do -

*Among many options, here is a standard recommendation:

Ah! _____   cro-ce de-li-zia, al   cor! _____

120

The cut is traditional for stand-alone performances of the aria.

[Ah, si!] Gio -

ir, gio - ir! [Ah!]_____

Tempo I (♩. = 84)

assai brillante

Sem - pre li - be - ra ____ deg - g'i - o fol - leg -

gia - re di gio - ia in gio - ia, vo' che scor - ra il vi - ver

Me voilà seule… Comme autrefois

from
LES PÊCHEURS DE PERLES

Georges Bizet

(She looks around, scared)

seule __ en ce lieu dé - sert où rè - gne le si - len - ce.

suivez **f** *a tempo*

f

Je fris - son - ne, j'ai peur,

(looking over the side of the terrace)

et le som - meil me fuit. Mais il est

fp **pp**

là; mon cœur __ de - vi - ne sa pré - sen -

suivez

Andante ♩. = 52

ce.

pp

p

Comme au - tre -

p

legato

fois _____ dans la nuit som - bre, ca - ché _____ sous le feuil-la-ge é -

135

Och, jaký žal!...Ten lásky sen

(Mařenka's Aria)

from

PRODANÁ NEVĚSTA (The Bartered Bride)

Bedřich Smetana

vě - řím, až s ním prom - lu vím.

Snad a - ni o tom ne - ví!

ó, — kýž se

mi v ne - sná - zi — té sku - teč - ná, sku - teč - ná — prav - da zje -

ví!

Moderato assai

dolce

Jak bla-hý ži-vot s mi-len-cem v snu tom-to jsem si přa - dla!

dolce *mf*

Tu o-sud při-vál vi-chři-ci a rů-že lá - sky sva-dla.

con affetto *(as if waking)* *affettuoso, poco accel.*

Ne, ne-ní mož-ný ta-ký klam, ne, ne, ne, ne, ne, ne - ní,

f *più moto* *accel.* *ff*

doloroso, poco languentando

ne-ní mož-ný ta-ký klam! Tent' smut-nou by byl ra-nou,

Klänge der Heimat
(Csárdás)
from
DIE FLEDERMAUS

Johann Strauss

147

im - mer dar _____ ganz al - lein _ ge - weiht! O Hei - mat, so _ wun - der - bar, wie strahlt dort die _ Son - ne so klar! Wie grün _ dei - ne Wäl - der, wie la - chend die Fel - der, o Land, wo so glück - lich ich war! Feu - er, _ Le-bens-lust,

schwellt ech - te Un - gar - brust, Heil! _____ Zum _ Tan - ze _ schnell,

Csár - dás tönt so hell! _____ Brau - nes _ Mäg - de - lein,

musst mei - ne Tänz'- rin sein; Reich _____ den _ Arm ge - schwind,

dun - kel - aü - gig Kind! _____ Zum Fie - del - klin - gen, _

*

mf

* optional cut to **

greift zum Be - cher, lasst ihn krei - sen, lasst ihn

krei - sen schnell von Hand zu Hand! Schlürft das Feu - er

im To - kay - er, bringt ein Hoch aus dem____

____ Va - ter - land! Ha!____

A Simple Sailor Lowly Born

from
HMS PINAFORE

Arthur Sullivan

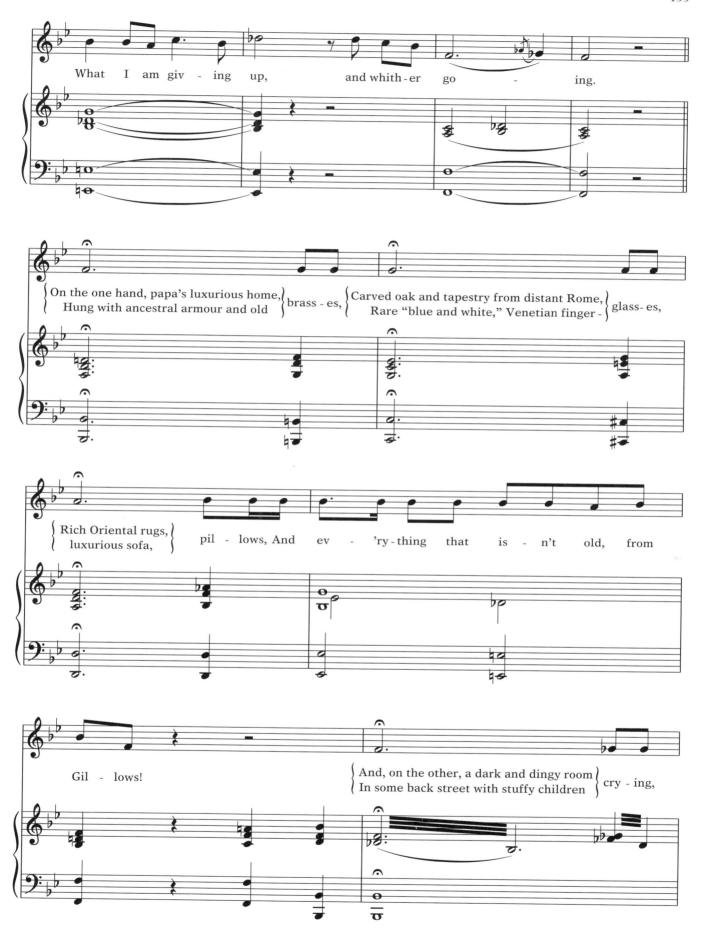

What I am giv - ing up, and whith - er go - ing.

On the one hand, papa's luxurious home,
Hung with ancestral armour and old { brass - es, { Carved oak and tapestry from distant Rome,
Rare "blue and white," Venetian finger - } glass- es,

Rich Oriental rugs,
luxurious sofa, } pil - lows, And ev - 'ry - thing that is - n't old, from

Gil - lows! And, on the other, a dark and dingy room
In some back street with stuffy children } cry - ing,

Where organs yell, and clacking housewives
fume, And clothes are hanging out all day a- dry - ing,

With one cracked looking-
glass to see your face in, And

dinner served up
in a pudding - bas-in!

Allegro con spirito

cresc. molto f

A sim - ple sail - or, low - ly born, Un-

let - tered and un - known, Who toils for bread from ear - ly morn Till

half the night has flown, Till half the night has flown! No

gold - en rank can he im-part, No wealth of house or land, No

cresc.

for - tune, save his trust - y heart, And hon - est, brown right hand, his trust - y

heart, and brown right hand! And yet he is so won - d'rous fair, That

Il est doux, il est bon
from
HÉRODIADE

Jules Massenet

Il est doux, ___ il est bon, ___ sa pa - role _ est se - rei - ne:

Il par - le... tout se tait; ___ Plus lé - ger _ sur la plai - ne

l'air at - ten - tif pas - se sans bruit; il par -

- le! Ah! quand re - vien - dra - t-il?

Tempo I

Il est doux, ___ il est bon, ___ sa pa - role est se -

rei - ne: Il par - le... tout se tait; ___

Plus lé - ger ___ sur la plai - ne l'air at - ten - tif

pas - se sans bruit; il par - - le!

168

Je suis encor
from
MANON

Jules Massenet

poco rall.
a tempo
pp
rall.

Je suis — en - cor tout é - tour - di - e!

poco rall.
a tempo
pp
colla voce

a tempo
(delivered in a lively manner)
f
p dolce

Par - don - nez à mon ba - var - da - ge, J'en suis à mon prem-ier voy - a -

f a tempo
p

a tempo
(faster than at the beginning)

ge!

a tempo
(faster than at the beginning)
f
sf

(in narrative fashion)

Le co - che s'é - loi-gnait à pei - ne, que j'ad-mi-rais de tous mes

eu - se, que je par-tais pour le cou-vent, pour le cou-vent, pour le cou -

vent! De - vant tant de cho - ses nou -

vel - les, ne ri - ez pas, si je vous dis que je croy -

ais a - voir des ai

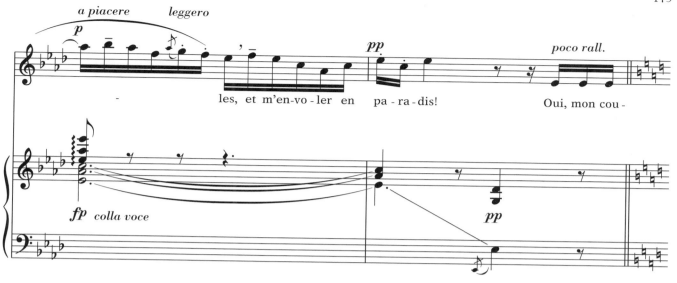

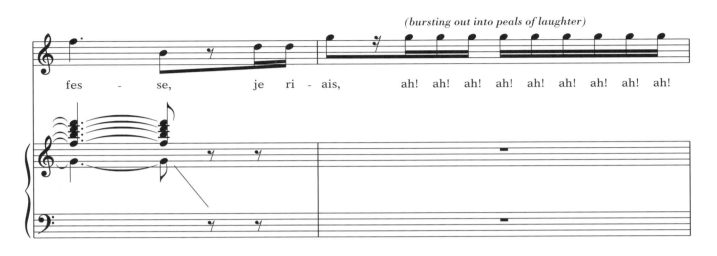

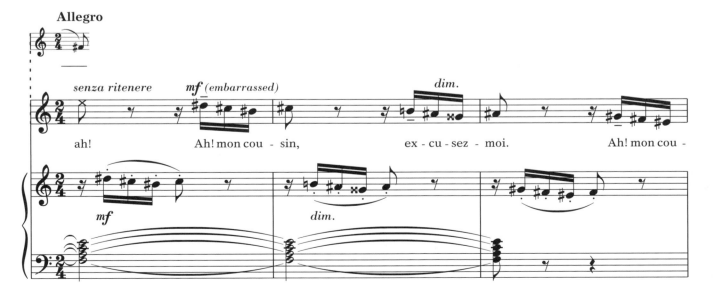

Obéissons quand leur voix appelle
(Gavotte)
from
MANON

Jules Massenet

Allegro moderato

Allegro maestoso ♩. = 72
(with impertinence and gaiety)

Je mar-che sur tous _ les __ che-mins _____

aus - si bien qu'u - ne __ sou - ve-rai -

(The 3rd beat in the 9/8 measure should be faster than the other two.)

- ne; on s'in-cli - ne, on bai - se mes mains, _____

* optional beginning

car par la beau-té je suis rei - ne, je suis

rei - ne! Mes _ che-vaux cou-rent _ à _ grands pas; _

de-vant ma vie a - ven - tu-reu -

- se, les grands s'a-van - cent cha - peau bas; _

ai - mons, __ ri - ons, chan-tons sans ces - se, nous n'a-vons en-core que __ vingt

Tempo primo
(Moderato e leggero)

ans! Ah! ah! Le

cœur, __ hé - las, le plus fi - dè - le, Ou-bli - e en un jour l'a - mour, __

__ l'a - mour, __ l'a - mour, Et la jeu-nes-se ou-vrant son ai - le a dis - pa

Ebben?... Ne andrò lontana

from

LA WALLY

Alfredo Catalani

Frère! voyez!... Du gai soleil

from
WERTHER

Jules Massenet

Animé et léger ♩. = 112

SOPHIE: *(gaily, to Albert)*

Frè - re! voy - ez!... Voy -

ez _____ le beau bou - quet! J'ai

(observing Werther and lightly scolding him)

Ah! le som - bre vi - sa - ge!

sf

(naïvely and with pointed politeness)

Mais au - jour - d'hui, mon-sieur Wer - ther,

p *dim.* *p*

tout le monde est joy - eux! Le bon-heur est dans

3

l'air!

pp

eux! Le bon-heur est dans l'air!

doux

Et l'oi - seau qui monte aux cieux dans la

rall.

Premier Mouvement subit

pp

bri - se qui sou - pi - re est re - ve - nu

pour _ nous di - re que

In quelle trine morbide

from
MANON LESCAUT

Giacomo Puccini

vez - za ___ a u -na ca - rez - za vo - lut -tu - o - sa di lab-bra ar -

den - ti e d'in-fuo -ca - te brac - cia or ho ___ tut-t'al-tra

co - sa! ___ O mia di -mo -ra u - mi -

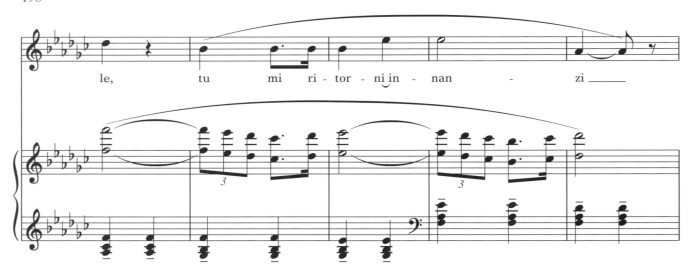

le, tu mi ri-tor-ni in-nan - zi ____

ga-ia, i - so-la - ta, bian - ca ____ co-me un so-gno gen-

ti - le e di pa - ce e d'a - mor!

Dis-moi que je suis belle
from
THAÏS

Jules Massenet

Tous ces hom-mes ne sont qu' in-dif - fé - ren - ce et _

_ que bru-ta-li -té.

Les fem-mes sont mé-chan - tes... et les heu-res pe -

san - tes! J'ai l'â - me vi - de... Où trou-ver le re -

pos? Et com - ment fix - er le bon-heur?

a mirror and contemplates her image)

Un jour, ____ ain-si, Tha-ïs

(with alarm)
ne se-rait plus Tha-ïs!

$(\text{♩.} = 63)$

très chanté et expressif

(calming, little by little)
Non! Non! je n'y puis croi - re!

(addressing Venus) *expressif*
Toi, Vé - nus, ____ ré - ponds-moi de ma beau -

cresc.

Depuis le jour
from
LOUISE

Gustave Charpentier

209

Měsíčku na nebi hlubokém

(Song to the Moon)
from
RUSALKA

Antonín Dvořák

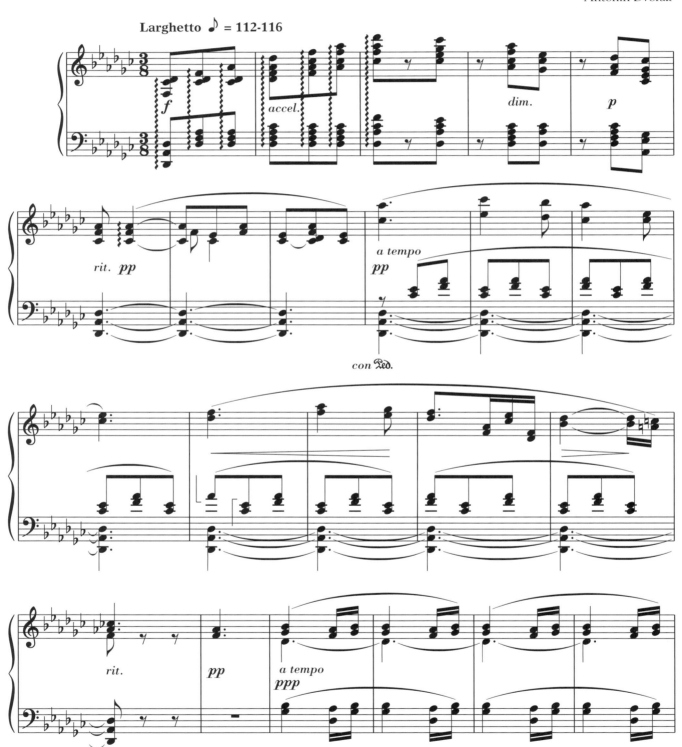

216

díváš se v příbytky lidí,

po světě bloudíš širokém,

díváš se v příbytky lidí.

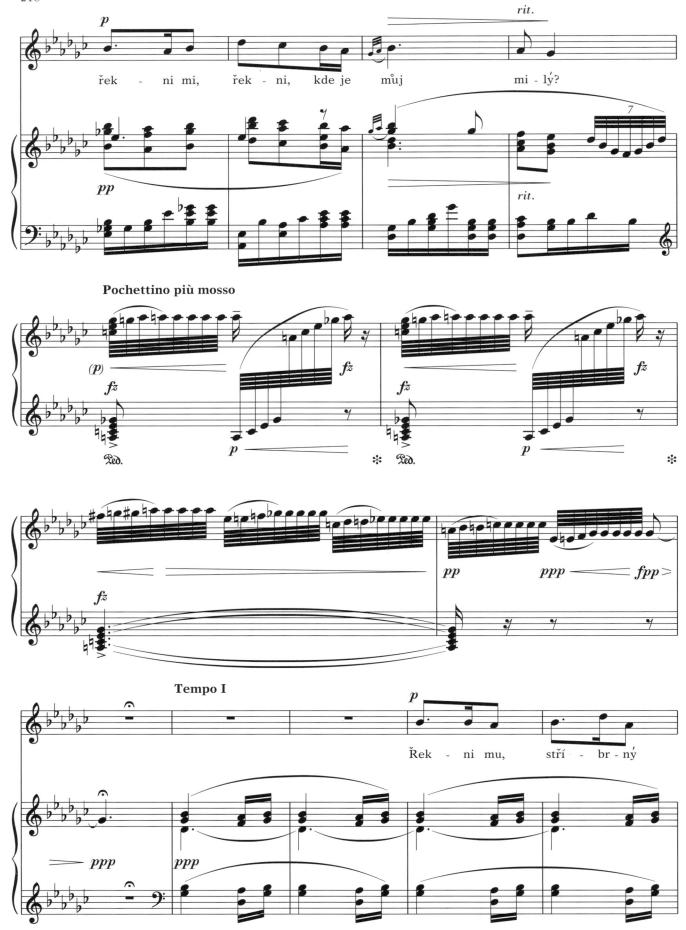

řek - ni mi, řek - ni, kde je můj mi - lý?

Pochettino più mosso

Tempo I

Řek - ni mu, stří - br - ný

mě - sí - čku, mé že jej ob - jí - má

pp

rá - mě, a - by si a - le - spoň

rit. a tempo

chvi - li - čku vzpo - me - nul ve sně - ní

mf pp rit. a tempo

na mne, a - by si a - le - spoň

mf *rit. poco a poco* *p* *rit.*

chvi - li - čku vzo - me - nul ve sně - ní

mf *pp* *p* *pp*
rit. poco a poco *rit.*

Ped. ✳ Ped. ✳

a tempo

na mne. Za - svěť mu do da-le-ka,

p
a tempo

Es lebt' eine Vilja
(Vilia)
from
DIE LUSTIGE WITWE

Franz Lehár

English version by Martha Gerhart

Im Volksliedton vorgetragen

1. Es lebt' ei - ne Vil - ja, ein Wald - mäg - de -
1. There once was a Vi - lia, a wood - mai - den
(2.) Wald mägd-lein streck - te die Hand nach ihm
(2.) wood - mai den si - lent - ly nod - ded her

f *pp* langsamer

lein, ein Jä - ger er-schaut' sie im Fel - sen-ge -
fair. She lived, long a - go, in a dark for - est
aus und zog ihn hin - ein in ihr fel - si - ges
head and drew him with - in to her dark fo - rest

stein! Dem Bur - schen, dem wur - de so ei - gen zu
lair. A - long came a hunts - man she stopped to be -
Haus. Dem Bur - schen die Sin - ne ver - gan - gen fast
bed. She kissed and ca - ressed him as no mor - tal

p

an?   Bang   fleht   ein   lieb -   kran -   ker   Mann!
why,   *in*   *your*   *em* -   *bra* -   *ces,*   *I*   *die!*

Sehr langsam
ppp   (opt. 2nd time)

Vil -   ja,   o   Vil -   ja,   was   thust   du   mir
Vi -   *lia,*   *oh*   *Vi* -   *lia,*   *will*   *love*   *tell*   *me*

ppp

Chi il bel sogno di Doretta

(La Canzone di Doretta)
from
LA RONDINE

Giacomo Puccini

do - vi - nar? Il suo mi - ster co - me mai, co - me mai fi -

nì?_____ Ahi - mè! un gior - no u - no stu - den - te in boc - ca

la ba - ciò, e fu quel ba - cio ri - ve - la - zio - ne:

Senza mamma

from
SUOR ANGELICA

Giacomo Puccini

a tempo, ma ben sostenuto

O o - ra che sei un an - ge - lo del cie - lo,

pp legato

o - ra tu puoi ve - der - la la tua

mam - ma! Tu puoi scen - de - re giù pel fir - ma -

calando, senza affrett.

men - to

pp

Un poco meno, sostenendo

ciar - ti?... O dol - ce fi - ne d'o - gni mio do -

lo - re, quan - do in cie - lo con te po - trò sa -

li - re?... Quan-do po-trò mo - ri - re?

Quan - do po - trò mo - ri - re, po - trò mo -

Calmo

Glück, das mir verblieb
(Marietta's Lied)
from
DIE TOTE STADT

Erich Wolfgang Korngold

Ich ken -

espress.

- ne das Lied. _____ Ich hört ___

p

___ es oft _____ in jun -

poco rit.

poco rit.

Di nuovo assai lento, con profonda espressione

246

Lentissimo (Adagio)

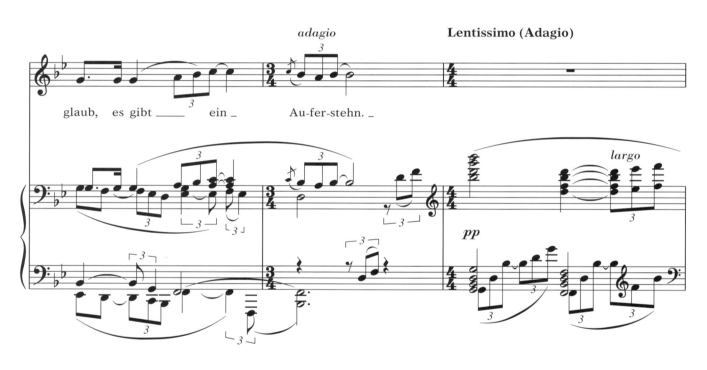

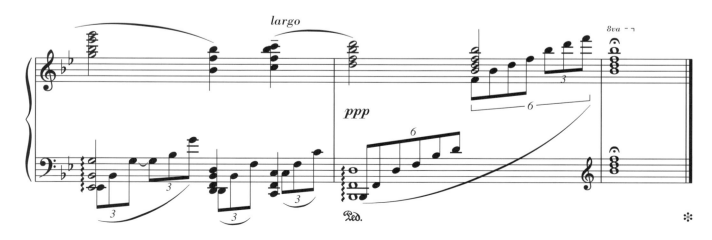

Dearest Mama
from
THE BALLAD OF BABY DOE

Douglas Moore

Allegro moderato

Meno mosso

stay to-geth - er. Ma-ma dear, ___ you oft-en told me ___ that I was

beau-ti - ful, ___ And that my beau - ty ___ de-served to find ___ a man some day so

rich, ___ a man so pow-er-ful, ___ that he could give me an - y-thing and make ___ me like a

prin - cess in old-en days. ___ Ah ___ Ah ___ And so I

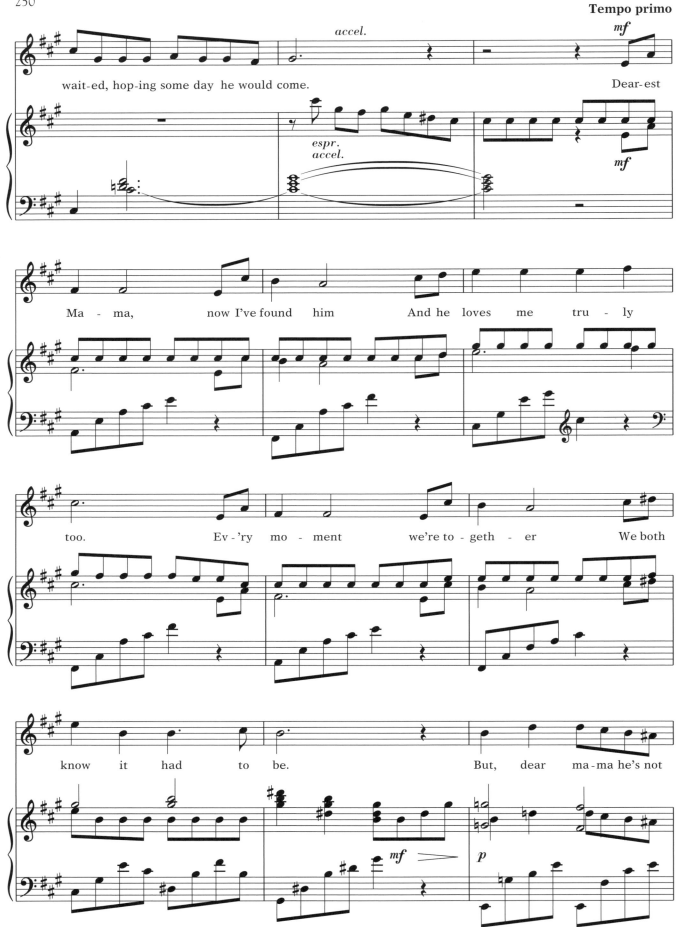

free to mar - ry. It is wrong for us to feel the way we do. I know he

needs me _____ and that I love him, But I have to give him up and we must

part for - ev - er, for - ev - - - er, for -

ev - - er. _____

I want magic!
from
A STREETCAR NAMED DESIRE

André Previn